Nollaig 2023

Nollaig shona duit dearthair
mo chroí!

Le grá, dílseacht agus
cairdeas

Caitlín x.

Dear Gay

Dear Gay

COMPILED BY SUZY BYRNE

Letters to *The Gay Byrne Show* –
A Handwritten History of Ireland

GILL BOOKS

Gill Books
Hume Avenue
Park West
Dublin 12
www.gillbooks.ie

Gill Books is an imprint of M.H. Gill and Co.

9780717195633

The letters reproduced in this book were all real letters written by real people to *The Gay Byrne Show*. In some instances, details have been changed and some handwritten letters have been rewritten to protect the letter-writer's identity.

Designed by Graham Thew Design
Print origination by Sarah McCoy
Printed and bound by Firmengruppe APPL, Germany
This book is typeset in Futura PT and Prestige Elite.

The paper used in this book comes from the wood pulp of sustainably managed forests.

A CIP catalogue record for this book is available from the British Library.

5 4 3 2 1

For all those who put pen to paper to write to Gay, and in particular for those who had the courage to share difficult stories at a time when so many remained unspoken. Your letters and stories changed Ireland for the better. We all owe you a debt of gratitude.

For Gay, the broadcaster, who gave so many the platform to speak and, in doing so, lifted us all higher.

For Dad, whom we loved beyond measure. As children, you made us feel part of your broadcasting world, but you also protected us from the painful realities you were uncovering.

For Mum, his and our rock through it all. Without you, none of this would have been possible.

Finally, for Ronan, Cian, Sadhbh and Saoirse – you are my world.

CONTENTS

—

The First

Brendan Kennelly

(Written for the final *Gay Byrne Show* in 1998)

You were the first to let the people speak their minds
You listened to what each one had to say
In your patient, tolerant, critical way.
Responding when they raised enquiring hands
To speak of pain or fun, of loss or gain.
You encouraged Ireland to open up
To face the ghosts of darkness, let them rip,
Express the secret heart in sun and ice and rain.
You were a one-man university
Where all were welcome without paying a fee.
You gave us words, ideas, music, song,
Often you made us laugh out loud and long.
Beneath it all you searched for what was true.

Thank you for that.

But thank you most of all for being you.

Preface

—

WHEN MY FATHER, GAY BYRNE, died in November 2019, he left behind an incredible broadcasting legacy. In 2010, the *Irish Times* wrote that he was 'unquestionably the most influential radio and television man in the history of the Irish State'. But to me he was simply Dad, and Dad constantly refuted any suggestion that he may have initiated the radical social change that Ireland witnessed while he was at the helm of both *The Late Late Show* and *The Gay Byrne Show*. As historian and broadcaster John Bowman said: 'We had the good fortune that we had the right person in the right place at the right time, to play an exceptional role in late 20th-century Irish history.' As I have compiled this book over the last two years, I think that this is a more accurate reflection of my father and the role he played.

In 1988, when *The Gay Byrne Show* was celebrating 15 years on air, making it the longest-running radio show on RTÉ at the time, the daily audience of the show was 850,000 people – nearly 25 per cent of the entire country's population (3.5 million). Those were the days of mass listenership. In a study in the same year, Telecom Éireann monitored attempted calls to *The Gay Byrne Show* and logged 30,000 over each two-hour period the show was on air.

Communication between Gay and his listeners was the cornerstone of his radio show. They talked, he listened. He read out their letters on air, and the letters in response would arrive by the sackful. The truth in the letters was raw; the writing of them so often incredibly brave; the content not new but yet untold. Here, they felt, was a man whom they could trust, with whom they could share their troubles, problems, hopes and dreams – from the mundane to the taboo, moments of joy to moments of desperation. These were opinions and issues they might never have shared with their closest family and friends, but Gay's voice – his presence in homes nationwide – was so ubiquitous in their day-to-day lives that they felt they could trust him.

Letter writing is something of a lost art today – but people of all ages, education, religion, sexuality and gender wrote to Dad, and these letters have been collected and preserved in the RTÉ archives, where they remain today. Some letters recount simple, innocent moments of everyday life – the first blooms of spring or preparing the children for their return to school. But other letters read on air acted as a springboard for debate, resulting in a deluge of responses and sparking national conversations and movements, the cumulative effect of which was to lift the lid on a long-hidden truth: that all was not as it seemed. In reality, a modern Ireland was slowly emerging, and people were ready to talk about it.

The Gay Byrne Hour and, later, *The Gay Byrne Show* bore direct witness to almost unimaginable change in Irish life over a relatively short period of time.

Dad, Me, Mum and Crona at the launch of *The Time of My Life* in Dobbins' Bistro in Dublin in 1989.

Many people over the years have applauded, or even glorified, Dad for his role in this. As I pieced together this book – reading these letters, the show scripts, the various telephone messages and interviews – Dad's skill as a broadcaster was clearly evident, and I'm grateful to have got to know this side of him. But on reflection, I, too, have come to believe what my Dad always said about his work: it was not just his voice that made the show what it was, but, rather, his ability to understand that people want to hear other people's stories. People wanted to listen to each other, not to him.

It is his skill as a broadcaster that allows the letters in this book to shine. While this book contains only a selection of those in the RTÉ archives, I think they illustrate the openness and honesty that people showed him. It was through these brave people that he understood the extent of the changes afoot in this country. Through their letters and telephone calls, he was enabled to ask the hard questions. He knew they needed to be asked. He knew because people had told him, by hand, of their real, lived experiences.

Dad was neither perfect nor superhuman, but I believe that he was a man of integrity. He recognised that the show was, and always should be, about the listener or programme contributor. This caused endless frustration to journalists as they endeavoured to analyse him and uncover the 'real Gay'. He always found this quite amusing. His life was one of hard work – not only broadcasting six days a week. He went to the theatre often, both because he loved it and, more important, because he could talk about it on radio. He read every book that featured on the show, plus countless others – our house was always full of books – as well as the daily newspapers, both Irish and British. All of this in addition to raising our family with Mum and walking the hills of Howth. It was a hard-working but a simple life. There were no big revelations to write about. He had no desire for 'celebrity' nonsense – he had a job to do. And after he had done it, he was wrecked!

Our mother, also a broadcaster, was a huge supporter of Dad. They were an incredible team right to the end. She understood the business, its demands and stresses, and knew many of Dad's colleagues in RTÉ through her own career working there. I remember her calling one of her friends in the wardrobe department to see if they had a black tail that I could borrow for my role as the Cheshire Cat in *Alice and Wonderland*. That evening, Dad arrived home, bemused, with a big fat black tail. Mum stepped back from broadcasting to raise myself and Crona, something I am eternally grateful to her for now that I have my own family. We never needed keys to get in after school. She was always there with her famously delicious dinners waiting for us. We were lucky.

Mum has often said that the radio and television shows did not enter our home. She listened every morning and diligently watched *The Late Late Show* every weekend, but she had seen and heard it all, so there was no need to discuss it at home. She understood that when Dad came home, it was his sanctuary, a place to put the day behind him. He loved being at home. I've heard that many people expected us, as a family, to discuss all that had gone on in the programme that day as soon as he walked in the door. Dad found this so amusing and he would say: 'Why the surprise? I doubt every dentist comes home and starts into a big chat about teeth after a long day.'

Dad had a wonderful sense of humour, often very dry, too. He was the most engaging storyteller and would regularly have us hanging on every word, in stitches laughing around the table. The more we laughed, the more he did. He was incredibly social and engaging, particularly with his close group of friends with whom he was simply himself, and they treated him as such, not in the slightest bit hesitant about giving him a tea towel to muck in and dry the dishes after a dinner. He loved that.

Of course, I didn't see Dad as the Gay Byrne that people around the country watched. All my life, people have asked me what it was like to be Gay Byrne's daughter. The simple answer to that question has always been the same: I knew no different. Your dad is your dad and it had always been that way. His work was totally normalised in our everyday lives. Growing up, Dad always welcomed my sister and me into RTÉ and encouraged us to come in to the studio. We frequently wandered through the corridors of Montrose. The buzz there was so incredible – we loved it. We knew *The Late Late Show* set like our own home. We regularly stood by the doors as the audience entered the studio, with a huge basket, collecting money for the Gay Byrne Show Fund. We knew every person on the television and radio show teams, the cameramen and women, the floor managers, and they knew us. It was like a family. They knew Dad so well. They were sensitive to every move he made – even his silent cues, like moving into the audience to

Christmas shopping in Switzers on Grafton Street in the late seventies.

signal that he might be bringing an interview to a close earlier than scheduled. Dad was first and foremost a broadcaster. Keeping listeners listening and viewers watching was number one. He believed that the rest would follow, and it did.

Like all teenagers, I was mortified when trips into town or walks along Howth Head would be, to my mind, derailed by people thanking him for speaking about a particular topic or indeed wanting to share their thoughts. I do remember a touching gesture from a London black-cab driver who refused to take a fare from him after a long journey, as a thank you for all the entertainment he had given his family, who lived in Liverpool, over the years. There were so many incidents like that right up until he died. People for whom he had done something that was fairly innocuous to him, but huge for them. If he came into their restaurant, bar or business, they wanted to say thank you. The kindness of strangers is never-ending. It took well into adulthood for me to realise the full impact that Dad had made and the unique position that he filled.

Crowds lining the streets on the morning of Dad's funeral.

Nowhere was this impact clearer to me than the morning of Dad's funeral, as we travelled the familiar journey from Howth into town, finally ending in Marlborough Street and the Pro-Cathedral. It was stunning, comforting and overwhelming, all at the same time, to see so many people lining the streets of Dublin to say one final goodbye to a man many of them had never met, and yet all felt as if they knew or had some connection with him. Among them were Gardaí, the fire brigade, Howth RNLI coastguard and school children, all standing in uniform, all applauding as the hearse drove past. I will never forget it.

Dad fully appreciated the contribution of the teams who worked with him to the success of both shows. He was protective and totally supportive of them. People who had cut their teeth on his research and production teams were much sought after, but to poach from Dad was a brave move, and he would let them go only if he believed it was right for them – that a move would further their career in the best way. He regularly became their mentor throughout their careers and loved to offer advice and hear of their progress.

Dear Gay is not about Gay Byrne and his place in the history books. It is about the ordinary people who took time out of their day to write to him – the conduit, the listener, the ringmaster of a changing Ireland. In an interview with Olivia O'Leary, Dad himself said: 'To be able to listen, a broadcaster must allow silence. Leave people a moment or two to get their thoughts together.' This book is these people's stories – their lives. It is a handwritten history of Ireland. The radio shows, the letters and the phone calls were never about Gay; they were always about these people's stories. I hope that this book captures just some of that.

SUZY BYRNE, JULY 2023

RTE GUIDE

PROGRAMMES APRIL 28—MAY 4 :: Vol. 10 No. 17 ::: IRIS RADIO TELEFIS EIREANN, APRIL 27, 1973. PRICE 4p.

THE GAY BYRNE HOUR on radio; see inside

1

To Whom It May Concern ...

—

ON 2 FEBRUARY 1973, the first episode of a new radio show, *The Gay Byrne Hour*, accompanied by a jaunty upbeat jingle, 'Tico's Tune' by Manuel and the Music of the Mountains, which would quickly become its signature, began broadcasting from Donnybrook, Dublin 4, to homes around Ireland. Its host, Gay Byrne, had already been presenting *The Late Late Show* on Saturday nights on RTÉ One for over ten years. For many people, *The Late Late Show* had been one of their first experiences of television. While the introduction of television coincided with a loosening of traditional values, swathes of the population were still devout Catholics, proud of their firmly held views, and many were amazed by the content and issues now being beamed directly into and openly debated in their living rooms every week.

The 1970s was a significant, transitional period for the people of Ireland, coming down from the economic highs of the 1960s but yet to face the crippling economic recession of the early 1980s. Many areas of Irish life were beginning to take tentative steps towards modernisation. Just one month before Gay's first episode aired, in January 1973, Ireland officially joined the European Economic Community, signalling its ambition to take its place on the European and world stages, after fifty years of government policies that had seen the country defined, first and foremost, by its independence from Britain. At the same time, a new urban middle class had begun to emerge, as many young people left their rural hometowns and migrated to the country's cities in search of better education and employment opportunities. Increased international travel also meant that many people were encountering new cultures and lifestyles that, just a few years previously, wouldn't have been possible. This social change was soundtracked by the emergence of new Irish rock bands such as Thin Lizzy and Horslips, as well as a nascent punk rock movement, later spearheaded by the Boomtown Rats. It marked a departure from the strait-laced dancehalls and travelling showbands that had dominated the music culture of the 1950s and 1960s.

Despite the social change afoot, when he began to programme his new hour-long morning radio show, Gay was tasked with targeting Ireland's huge daytime audience of stay-at-home women and mothers. Many of these women stayed at home by choice, but many were legally prevented from working.

RTE GUIDE, APRIL 27, 1973   Three

When Gabriel calls...

Eanna Brophy notes the latest success of Gay Byrne on radio and talks to him about the appeal of "The Gay Byrne Hour," which is on the air, each morning, from Monday to Friday, at 10.01 a.m.

Gay Byrne in the RTE Radio studios . . . a new success with his morning radio show.

The Gay Byrne Hour was an instant hit with listeners around the country.

At the time, the marriage bar required many women to resign from their jobs once they married, and disqualified married women from applying for job vacancies. Though formally in force only within the civil service, the ban was in effect across both the public and the private sector. Additionally, since 1922, legislation had removed any widow's right to return to her civil service job on the death of her husband. The bar reflected social attitudes at the time: it was a husband's duty to support his wife, and a married woman's place was in the home. The ban was lifted in 1973, and even though any woman who had resigned now had the right to return to her old job, to actually get it back she had to show that she was no longer supported by her husband, whether due to desertion, illness or marital separation. In 1977, European law would make this discrimination illegal.

These women were incorrectly assumed to be uninterested in politics and current affairs, and so, instead, were to be entertained by a light blend of music, chat and requests. John Bowman once said that Gay 'had a surer sense of public opinion than the custodians of old Ireland'. While that may have been true as the years went on, Gay wasn't so sure in the beginning. The chatty style of this new show was a complete novelty. Prior to *The Gay Byrne Hour*, morning radio consisted of the news, and programmes with announcers reading out requests from listeners.

Nevertheless, he agreed to give it a go for a few months and see what sort of reaction he received. If things didn't work, it would be parked – no hard feelings. Once the show started broadcasting, it's safe to say that lack of interest, or content, was never a concern again ...

The RTÉ archives have very few letters kept from the early 1970s, but the letters in this chapter show an emerging Ireland. Daily running orders for the show illustrate that anything and everything could be covered. They give a flavour of the lighter side of *The Gay Byrne Show*, the wide variety of stories and issues that remained an important part of the programme throughout its 25 years, even as Gay and his listeners would tackle more difficult topics later on. According to Gay's first producer, Billy Wall, 'for the first year or more, it was basically a music programme', designed to appeal to the audience that he and Gay imagined: women with families, left by themselves for a few hours each morning, occupied with looking after their children and running their homes.

> "I keep asking for the rude letters about me or the programme and the simple fact is that they don't come in — unlike the Late Late Show where they're a regular feature."

The GAY BYRNE HOUR goes on air

Catherine Cronin meets the boys and girls who make this nationwide radio programme tick

How the mystery voice works . . . sifting through the requests . . . reading the letters . . . putting out the pleas for help.

IT STARTS quietly enough. By five minutes past nine the presenter Gay Byrne arrives, looking frozen. Producer Billy Wall is already in the studio, timing records. Bursts of the signature tune and strangled segments of ads can be heard as the sound-desk operator begins to run through his check-list. Gay Byrne, keeping his coat on until the central

WOMAN'S WAY, 4th MARCH, 1977

heating thaws him a little, sits at a round table in the studio and silently reads through several hand-written letters which will go on the air later on. Some are clearly written and easy to follow, but some look as if they have been written by an arthritic drunk in Chinese. In due course, he will read them as if they had been typed impeccably.

Mary the telephone girl

AT nine-fifteen Mary Martin arrives, carrying bundles of post and several newspapers for Gay. She is the "Mary" he advises people on the telephone to talk to if they want to qualify for a secondhand set of the Encyclopaedia Brittanica,

a brace of geese, or a chance at the Mystery Voice. She sits at the telephone which is already beginning to give half-hearted wasp noises, with a lapful of what turn out to be Mystery Voice guesses. This morning, it's the first chance at a new Mystery Voice, so there are relatively few. Normally,

TURN OVERLEAF

Way article fr . . . 1977 . . .

THE GAY BYRNE HOUR

FROM PREVIOUS PAGE

there are anything from two hundred and upwards every day.

She answers the telephone. "Gay Byrne Hour? No, I'm sorry. It's not possible to talk to himself at the moment. Could I help you?"

When the call finishes, Billy Wall glances questioningly at her.

"Lost dog," she says briefly. It's Monday and Monday's a big day for lost dogs.

"They bring their dogs out for a walk on Sundays," she explains, "and lose them, then want the Gay Byrne Hour to broadcast an appeal. You feel very sorry for them, but if we did that kind of thing, we'd simply never come to the end of it and," she adds as an after-

thought, "we don't give away litters of puppies either."

Mary works the early morning shift from seven o'clock until lunchtime, handling telephone calls and paperwork for a number of programmes of which the Gay Byrne Hour is one. It's probably the most hectic.

"You don't get a chance to breathe," she maintains. "For one thing, there are the dozens of listeners who want to check that their card offering their solution to the mystery voice has actually arrived. Then there are the callers who want to continue a controversy raised by the programme and there are the people who just want to let us know their views about something. I had one

woman on for forty minutes one morning who wanted to tell us her views on young people and the state of the world today. She'd written this big long song, all full of social comment — everything from the emancipation of women to the horrors of war and she put down her receiver on the piano and played away and sang the whole thing. People kept coming into the studio (we played it through the monitor) and asking was this some new record."

Countdown to blast-Off

THINGS begin to get a bit hectic. The monitor blurts out the noises of the telephone being tested. Gay has been put through to the Gay Byrne Hour office, one floor above, where Noreen Nichol, one of the two programme secretaries,

takes the call to make sure that the quality of the line is good enough for broadcast.

"Hi honey," Gay says, still sounding cold and a little tired, "I'm hearing you loud and clear."

"I can't hear you at all," Noreen says briskly and the technicians go to work to sort it out.

Billy Wall looking vague steps into the studio to discuss some of the morning's letters with Gay. The vague look is permanent and deceptive and as the programme proceeds, he turns out to be as vague as a guided missile, running his wheeled producer's chair back and forth at speed between the telephone and the microphone through which he communicates with Gay, making production decisions and cueing the man who spins the discs.

Just before air-time, Mary, using the back end of a biro in the telephone

"Hello. Can I help you?" Mary Martin the girl you talk to on the telephone.

Programme secretary Noreen Nichol takes the line is good enough for broadcasting.

Gay and Billy consult together on some matters of importance.

Programme secretary Niamh Kenny. "It's totally involved and responsible."

WOMAN'S WAY, 4th MARCH, 1977

dial, contacts the woman whose name has been picked from the cards in the big bag to make a guess at the Mystery Voice. She turns out to be so excited at the prospect of talking to Gay on the air that she thinks it will bring on her baby, due in a week's time.

This message is channelled through to Gay and for the first time he smiles and at the same time takes off his coat.

The commercial reader goes into the studio with his scriptful of ads and last-minute voice tests go on. The newsreader's voice percolates into the studio from continuity, reporting that driving conditions are hazardous.

"You could sing that if you had an air to it," says the man on the sound desk and rolls the signature tune. For a moment, I am slightly disappointed. For some crazy reason, I'd *always* assumed that the* hand-clapping in the cheery little sig was provided by Gay himself. It isn't.

On the air

THE signature fades and the Byrne voice, richer on the studio monitors than on home transistors takes over with a snippet freshly culled from a morning newspaper about a couple fired for making love in their lunch hour in Italy. As the first record of the morning slips in over his muttered comments, I ask the sound man about the almost casual hand-signals Byrne gives to cue in the music.

"For that kind of thing," says the sound man, as the Yetis belt out 'Cigareets and Whisky and Wild, Wild Women,' he's tops. He's just the best there is. His signals are on the button and he always does what he signals he's going to do — and he's undistractable."

Ribald comment continues in the control room concerning the Italian lovemaking story while Gay reads aloud the first letters of the morning, and broadcasts a plea from someone who has had a relative die in a country area, missed the train and needs transport.

Another record. Then three letters, about which Gay says he will make no comment. They are sad and personal reports of the grief of sexual frigidity and how it can damage a marriage.

As the music fades up following the last of them, I expect there to be comment and perhaps even laughter. There is none. Someone mutters "Gawd" with a mixture of sympathy and awe for the sufferers of the problem and the record spins to silence in the control room.

Telephone helpers and the mystery voice

BY THIS time Mary Martin has more or less lost touch with the programme, so busy is she answering the telephone on which dozens of callers are now queueing up. By half-past-ten, good news is beginning to filter through. Someone is prepared to lend a book, someone else has a suggestion for unkinking a record which was left in the sun and got warped, a third person says he's heading for the country area to which the earlier bereaved caller wanted a lift and that he'd be charmed to offer a lift, the pregnant guesser at the Mystery Voice is put through to Gay and gurgles agreeably when Gay suggests that the new

TURN OVERLEAF

a call to make sure that the quality of sound of

Everything under control . . . at work in the control room.

different from any other programme. You're so

Billy Wall's vague look is deceptive for he's about as vague as a guided missile.

THE GAY BYRNE HOUR

FROM PREVIOUS PAGE

arrival if it arrives that day, should be named after him.

Suddenly, the programme begins to feel like a bicycle on a steep slope. It hurtles towards its conclusion and as always, Gay times his "Good morning" to a split second, inserting it in a tiny gap of silence before the signature tune chortles to a halt.

The girls who sign the letters

FOR most people, that's the end of the Gay Byrne Hour for another day, for the two girls who sit facing each other in the office which handles all the programme's work, the Gay Byrne Hour really only begins at that point. Niamh Kenny and Noreen Nichol between them handle mountains of post and hundreds of telephone calls every day.

"It's very different from any other programme I was ever working on," Niamh explains. "You're just so totally involved and responsible."

By 'responsible' she means that the two girls advise callers when their calls cover areas which the programme can't handle, refer them to experts for particular problem and organise the transfer of various items from donors to recipients.

Replies to letters to the Gay Byrne hour often carry their signatures.

"I didn't like that at first," Noreen admits. "I hated to see my own name at the bottom of a letter."

Gradually, however, they found that through telephone and letter contact, they built up great numbers of 'friends' whom they rarely if ever meet. Now, they have particular friends among the social workers and other regular 'clients' of the programme. It's not surprising, when you watch them in action.

They deal every day with calls ranging from cries for material help to requests for aid with a marriage problem and their response manages to steer the delicate line between being full of concern for the callers and at the same time avoiding sentimentality.

The Gay Byrne Hour is, among other things, a social service. Niamh and Noreen spend their days mating offers of televisions, washing machines and bottled gas cookers with requests from deserving cases for the same things. They find marriage counsellors and other experts for people who need them and they have evolved the craziest filing system in the world. It just happens to make sense, they say, to have on the same file-card references to "Monologues, Millionaires and Models of shops," or "Heaters, hand bellows and handwriting experts."

Over coffee in the canteen after the programme, Gay Byrne and Billy Wall talk about the show and how it has evolved into a curious blend of highly popular entertainment and social service.

"We never really envisaged that it would have quite so much social content," Billy says.

"It just suddenly took off in the first weeks," Gays says. "The whole basis of this was that Billy wanted me to do the programme and I was unsure". "You were, really," Billy breaks in.

"And I said, "All right, let's try it for a couple of months and if we all fall out and become deadly enemies, we'll forget it and go back to where we were. Then it took off in the first fortnight."

That was just on five years ago. Since then, the programme has gone from strength to strength, gaining in popularity. Both presenter and producer feel that what they have in response to the Gay Byrne Hour is not just a larger audience than might have been expected, but a more attentive one.

"That's the extraordinary thing about it," Gay says. "We reckon they actually *listen* a lot more than they might."

"That's been borne out by surveys too," Billy puts in.

"It seems to us," Gay goes on, "that — no, we've been *told*, over and over again that women at home switch on the transistor and take it with them round the house and that they switch off vacuum cleaners and washing machines to actually listen."

The variety of the programme's content is one of the reasons for its success. The programme's planners are fairly ruthless. One request for a particular item, or one story on a theme is all that will be broadcast, although the office may receive dozens on the same lines. Billy Wall says simply that the programme is in the business of entertaining people and that however deserving subsequent offers on an already exploited theme may be, they can't be aired without boring the listeners. So far, the evidence is that the mixture as presented suits the vast bulk of them.

"I keep asking Billy for the rude letters about me or the programme," Gay says, "and the simple fact is they don't come in — unlike the Late Late Show, where they're a regular feature."

He explains that even when the Late Late Show has an outstandingly popular edition (as, for example, the special on Maureen Potter) there will be a couple of dozen telephone calls reviling him personally and the programme in general. This just doesn't happen with the Gay Byrne Hour. Just why, neither producer nor presenter is quite sure. All they know for sure is that it's overwhelmingly popular.

"Since the programme started, we have increased the listenership at ten o'clock by two hundred thousand," Billy offers. For him and the two girls, Niamh and Noreen, this means that from the time they come off the air until the programme goes on again next morning, they are dealing with a vast volume of correspondence which ideally, calls for a full-time social worker.

"What I think is most interesting," sums up Gay Byrne, "is that there are so many people in this country who don't know where to begin to find someone to help them with a problem and they pick a name out of the air like the Gay Byrne Hour or Billy Wall and write to us." ●

7.30 MORNING AIRS

Presented by **Liam Devally**, with music, news and traffic information. Contributors: **Philip Greene** and **Tom McCuaig**.

7.30 THE NEWS and WEATHER
7.33 A THOUGHT FOR THE DAY
Speaker **Pansy Boake**.
7.55 WEATHER FORECAST
Producer: **Colin Morrison**.

8.00 THE NEWS

and IT SAYS IN THE PAPERS

8.15 MORE MORNING AIRS

presented by **Liam Devally**.
8.30 NEWS HEADLINES
8.35 WEEKEND SPORTS RESULTS

9.00 THE NEWS

and IT SAYS IN THE PAPERS

9.15 ROGHA CEOIL

with **Vincent Bradley**.
9.30 NUACHT HEADLINES
Producer: **Colin Morrison**.

10.00 NEWS SUMMARY

10.01 THE GAY BYRNE HOUR

Gay Byrne invites you to join him after breakfast for some music. Featured today are: the songs of **Gordon Lightfoot**, a round-up of the new films and the Mystery Sound competition.

10.30 NUACHT HEADLINES
Producer: **Billy Wall**.
(See page 3)

10.58 A THOUGHT FOR THE DAY

(Repeat)

11.00 NEWS HEADLINES

11.01 HERE AND NOW

Current affairs, people and the arts.
11.30 (approx.) NUACHT HEADLINES
12.00 THE ANGELUS
12.01 NEWS HEADLINES
12.03 LETTERS FROM LISTENERS
12.30 NUACHT HEADLINES
12.50 (approx.) AR BHEAGAN GAEILGE
Presenter: **Liam Nolan**.
Reporter: **Freda McGough**.
Producers: **Michael O'Donnell, Brian Reynolds** and **Maxwell Sweeney**.
Music Producer: **John Keogh**.
Editor: **Howard Kinlay**.

12.59 NEWS HEADLINES

5.00 NEWS HEADLINES

5.01 THE YOUNG ENTERTAINERS

(S)
Proinsias O Ceallaigh introduces the Irish Youth Orchestra, conducted by **Hugh Maguire**, in the second of two programmes recorded at a Concert in the RDS, Dublin, on Thursday, January 4.
Producer: **Jane Carty**.

5.30 MUSIC ON THE MOVE

Valerie McGovern presents music, comment and information to ease the tensions of the rush hour.
5.55 WEATHER FORECAST
6.00 THE ANGELUS
6.01 AN NUACHT
6.10 (approx.) SPORTSNEWS
Producer: **Roisin Lorigan**.

6.30 THE NEWS

The latest home and foreign news followed by **Roundabout**—a look at local happenings all over Ireland presented by **Kevin MacDonald**.
6.55 (approx.) LIVESTOCK PRICES AND STOCK EXCHANGE

7.00 EUROPEAN POP JURY

Larry Gogan at Seezer's Discotheque presides over the home jury in an international record and voting session in which groups of young people in **Germany, Ireland, Norway, Sweden, Britain** and **Yugoslavia** express their approval (or otherwise) of current hits from each other's pop charts.
Introduced from London by **David Gell**.
Producer: **Adavin O'Driscoll**.

8.00 NUACHT HEADLINES

8.01 IMPRINT

A view of the world of books featuring tonight: "Irish Unionism 2" by **Patrick Buckland**, reviewed by **Roy Bradford**, M.P., "Group Portrait," by **Lady Ivy Heinrich Boll**, reviewed by **Benedict Kiely**, "My Own Story" by **an tAthair Peadar O Laoghaire**, translated by **Sheila O'Sullivan**, reviewed by **Ciaran Mac Mathuna** "The Black Book" by **Lawrence Durrell** reviewed by **Kevin Casey**.
Presented by **Seamus Heaney**.
Producer: **Kieran Sheedy**.

8.30 THE SOUND OF THE LIGHT

The RTE Light Orchestra under the baton of **Robert Murphy**, presents a medley of melody, rhythm and special orchestrations featuring **Tina** and **Davy Martin**.
Compere: **Val Joyce**.
Producer: **Johnny Devlin**.

A radio schedule from the early 1970s, published in the *RTÉ Guide*.

This call-out for the programme, provisionally titled 'Gay Calling', gives a good indication of the type of material that Gay planned to cover.

> Every morning at around about ten o'clock, Gay Byrne will be in the studio to present sixty minutes of records with a bright and happy sound … Items on the show will include news about books, cars, and films, the mystery sound competition …

Gay also sought audience participation. He was interested in people and their stories, and he wanted to hear about what mattered to them in their day-to-day lives. Writing in the *Irish Times*, journalist Mick Heaney wrote: 'If Byrne's strength as host of *The Late Late Show* was his willingness to talk about controversial subjects, his greatness on radio was down to his ability to listen.' *The Gay Byrne Hour* was the first Irish radio programme to invite listeners to contribute to the show interactively, to talk about whatever was on their minds and what was important to them. In an interview in 2001, Gay spoke of how he had to fight to use telephones live on air. The reason he fought so hard was that he believed that 'people who want to tell you things, if they are sitting in the studio, they are inhibited by the paraphernalia, lights, headphones, et cetera. When they are sitting in their own hall, their own kitchen, their own home, they are much more likely to be intimate about it and confessional about it.' Today, the practice is commonplace in Irish radio, but at the time it was revolutionary. This call-out shows the efforts that Gay and his producers went to when encouraging listeners to contact the show:

> If there is a piece of music which reminds you of a significant time in your life, Gay will be glad to hear why the record means so much to you. You may have been on a holiday abroad and every time you hear a certain piece of music you immediately associate it with the good time you had. Why not write to Gay Byrne about it and he will read your letter and play the record.

> Each morning Gay will make a phone greeting to somebody who is celebrating a birthday or an anniversary. If you or your friends are having a special occasion, why not drop a card to Gay telling him about it and he may phone you during the course of the programme.
>
> If you have a friend or acquaintance with whom you have lost contact and whom you are anxious to trace, you should write … and Gay will try to bring you together again.

In a world as yet unconnected by the internet or social media, radio was a lifeline for so many. In the days before local radio, RTÉ Radio 1 was the nation's town hall. *The Gay Byrne Show* had upwards of 850,000 daily listeners – these were the days of mass audiences, before they were diluted by commercial stations and increased choice. While Gay welcomed the conversation and interaction between himself and his listeners, he also understood that his listeners were in conversation with each other. In many ways, he saw himself as a link, a conduit, an inquisitor and a messenger all in one – for a spread-out community all connected through the radio.

The only ways of contacting Gay – indeed, the only forms of communication across the country – were by phoning or writing a letter. It wasn't long before the RTÉ radio centre began to receive huge bags of letters, all marked for Gay's attention – and sometimes addressed simply to 'Mr Gay Byrne, Dublin'. They all began with the same greeting: *Dear Gay.*

The vast majority of the show's early letters were light-hearted – simple observations, anecdotes and humorous quips written as people went about their day. In a later interview on the early years, Gay recounted, 'we specialised in finding things for people'. Many of the early letters and call transcripts that I came across in the archives ask Gay for help in procuring difficult-to-find items and services, looking for advice and recommendations from his other listeners – from things as innocent as 'a nice, soft, bouncy double bed' to other, more pressing items. Take, for example, this solemn request:

A young married man died recently in tragic circumstances, leaving behind a young family. This family have been unable to trace his will but feel that it may be inside the cover of an important historical book on the life of Daniel O'Connell. The name of the book is:

The Liberator [Author, a Kenmare nun]

The dead man either loaned or sold the book in the last six months approximately.

This family are not interested in the return of the book but would be most grateful to anyone who came into possession of a copy of the book recently, if they thumbed through the book to search for the missing will.

Note: Book is about four inches thick - leather cover with clasp. Edges of pages are gilded.

While going through the archives in RTÉ, I couldn't help but smile at some of the dilemmas that Gay and his team helped to resolve. On one Wednesday morning episode in 1986, Gay spoke to Christine. She had called in to tell Gay about how her artificial left hand had been stolen, and she asked him and his listeners for help. Just two days later, Gay took great pleasure in being able to tell his audience: 'Well, no sooner said than done! Christine rang us this morning to say she collected her artificial hand from the Gardaí in Store Street yesterday. It was handed in by an old man who found it in a block of flats in Dublin's city centre. He heard her appeal on our programme and promptly handed it in. Christine would like to thank this old man and all our listeners who very kindly offered to help her.'

This relationship with women formed the foundation of the radio show, and it would continue for the entirety of the show's 25-year run. As evident from the archives, the running orders of each show illustrate the variety of topics that would jump from serious to light-hearted and hilarious, often several times within the one show. Even years later, when the show was regularly airing more controversial subjects, Gay never wanted to lose sight of the show's roots. He continued trying to help people find missing items, no matter how unusual.

DETAILS

A YOUNG MARRIED MAN DIED RECENTLY IN TRAGIC CIRCUMSTANCES LEAVING BEHIND A YOUNG FAMILY.

THE FAMILY HAVE BEEN UNABLE TO TRACE HIS WILL, BUT FEEL THAT IT MAY BE INSIDE THE COVER OF AN IMPORTANT HISTORICAL BOOK ON THE LIFE OF DANIEL O'CONNELL

THE NAME OF THE BOOK IS

"THE LIBERATOR -- AUTHOR {A KENMARE NUN}

THE DEAD MAN EITHER LOANED, SOLD ~~OR LEFT~~ THE BOOK IN THE LAST SIX MONTHS APPROXIMATELY.

THE FAMILY ARE NOT INTERESTED IN THE RETURN OF THE BOOK, BUT WOULD BE MOST GRATEFUL TO ANYONE WHO CAME INTO POSSESSION OF A COPY OF THE BOOK RECENTLY, IF THEY THUMBED THROUGH THE BOOK TO SEARCH FOR THE MISSING WILL.

NOTE   BOOK IS ABOUT 4 INCHES THICK -
LEATHER COVER WITH CLASP.
EDGES OF PAGES ARE GILDED.

Dear Gay,

We all love the programme, keep up the good work.

Can you help me, Gay? I'm desperate. This is not a joke. I always wear a certain bra but Playtex took my size off the market. I have tried so many different types but hopeless. (I have a collection of them.)

Gay, I have written to Playtex in Scotland, but they sent me a list of their garments. I have tried various shops in Tipp, Clonmel, Limerick, Tuam and Dublin but to no avail.

Perhaps if you look for one on your show, some shop may have one in old stock. My size is 36 D (or 38 D). Playtex, no. 173. Thanks, Gay, for listening to my problem. I hope some of your listeners can help.

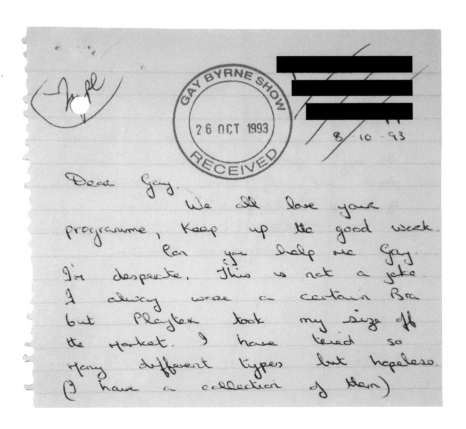

Pope John Paul II visited Ireland in 1979.

Ireland in the 1970s was still a deeply Catholic country. Records from the time suggest that over 90 per cent of the population attended church weekly, and this was to remain almost as high throughout the subsequent decade. Going through the letters across such varied themes, it's interesting to see how so many of the letters are imbued with an awareness of the teachings of the Catholic Church. Much of the correspondence uncovered from the archive may, today, seem incredibly innocent, but it's important to keep in mind that, directly or indirectly, religion was a major contributing factor to how many Irish people perceived and interacted with the world, and it continued in this way for many decades. Unusual circumstances were viewed suspiciously and, in turn, superstitiously – as seen in this concerned query.

> For the past six months, little birds have been coming into the house from the garden. They're little finches and tits, and they are totally fearless. They just ignore us and come on in. I didn't mind this at all until friends and relations and even the parish priest said that birds coming into the house are a sign of death for the household.
>
> I didn't mind them until I heard that. A relation said to sprinkle holy water out the back door and that would get rid of them. I keep telling the children that Saint Francis of Assisi was a great friend of the birds … that they never brought him bad luck, and look what happened to him!
>
> Does anyone know about this 'death sign' thing? It's a bit worrying.

How listeners responded reveals something of the Ireland of the time. Thankfully, according to this particular listener, there's nothing to worry about, but a portentous undertone remains:

> I don't think it's the birds coming into the house that are alive that are the unlucky sign, but if she discovered a dead bird. This happened to a friend of mine.

She woke up one morning to find a dead bird on her
windowsill and that day her sister died.

It's easy to forget that this was a time before the answer to any question was instantly at our fingertips. But if you had a tricky question, you could always ask Gay, as this panicked caller did in relation to their Christmas preparation:

I put in my Christmas cake in the oven yesterday at 1 p.m.
and the electricity went off at 1.45 p.m. I rang [a nearby
cookery school] and they said not to continue cooking
because the fruit will sink to the bottom, but some
neighbours said I could restir the cake and start again.
Would anyone be able to tell me the best thing to do?

Hopefully, some kindly and knowledgeable listener took the time to send a helpful response, as one thing I know for sure: Dad would not have had the slightest notion of how to answer this one!

Naturally, given his predominantly female audience, Gay was especially attuned to the concerns of women. He had a way with them – a charm and a warmth that would instantly put them at ease. He had a habit of calling them 'honey' when speaking to them on the phone. Dad firmly believed that the success of the radio show was in its ability to decipher the real issues on the ground, the issues being brought to his attention through the letters that came from the combined efforts – much of it unspoken – of a great number of women who supported him throughout his life.

In our own home, Dad lived among women. While the day-to-day of *The Late Late Show* and *The Gay Byrne Show* didn't enter our home per se, my mother's opinions and feedback were hugely important to Dad – he knew they were honest. I remember this more in relation to *The Late Late Show* than the radio. Mum would always watch, and if she felt something didn't work, she would tell him. I'm sure this was the same for the radio, too. They were both broadcasters, so she understood. She also represented so many of the show's listeners: a woman and a mother who had herself been affected by so many of the issues being discussed.

Our own home was Dad's haven and refuge. He worked incredibly hard and often came home totally drained. The drive from Montrose to Howth was his peace at the end of long days. At the time, we were children, so were more or less oblivious to both the radio and television shows, but later I understood the peace he adored in the car, his need to head out for an hour's walk to clear his head, and ready himself for the chatter of us girls. We always felt he loved coming home. Routine was so important to him. He couldn't bear chaos – he was a list man. Every evening he would come home, go straight to the television set and, one by one, place his diary, wallet, comb, keys and rosary ring on top of the TV, from where he would take each, one by one, the next morning. He had a deep faith since his childhood, and though he never really talked about religion with us as such, he carried a rosary ring which had been given to him as a gift. He had been educated at the Christian Brothers in Synge Street – prayers and the catechism learned by rote. Although we never said prayers at home, he often amusingly recounted his horror at me once asking him what the prayer the 'Memorandum' was, rather than the 'Memorare'. He assumed that religion was being taught to us at school – not very well, on that evidence!

Our grandmother, Dad's mother, was a formidable and important presence in his life. A daily Mass-goer, she had a deep faith, and she was organised and hard-working – qualities which certainly rubbed off on Dad. She was typical of so many housewives at the time. Dad always said that, in another time and place, she might have run her own business, but, 'not having the opportunity, she substituted her family and ran it with success and expansion in mind'. She believed that education was the route to self-improvement and was determined that Dad, along with his brothers and sister, Mary, would go to secondary school, something that wasn't a given back in those days. These women, along with those who wrote to Gay, consciously or unconsciously, influenced the direction and content of his show.

Within the halls of RTÉ, Dad was continually supported by a small army of women on both his radio and television teams; and, while the teams changed over the years, the input of many talented researchers, both male and female, was key to the show's success. Among the women were Maura Connolly, his long-time special assistant, and June Levine, whom Dad credited with educating him about women

Gay and the small army it took to produce his shows.

and about the feminist movement. To him, as he publicly said, all these women were his key educators and supporters of his principal audience.

Of the researchers on both *The Late Late Show* and *The Gay Byrne Show* over the years, Gay said: 'All of those people, and there were many who made no small contribution to the success of the programmes, and as the one constant north star among them, I owe them a debt of gratitude.'

Dad himself was a product of the Ireland of the time: values of integrity, hard work and responsibility towards others were ingrained in him. He had also experienced the harsh treatment of children at the hand of power during his education with the Christian Brothers, and probably from that time, he understood that the stories contained in later letters about this could be true. Gay forged his relationship with listeners initially through mundane everyday items such as the weekly shopping basket, discussing cures for snoring, fielding complaints about smelly husbands and finding things for people. This, though, was the bedrock that empowered them to write about darker subjects.

One woman who tuned in every day was Catherine Corless. In the early years of *The Gay Byrne Hour*, she was a full-time mother looking after her four children.

'What I loved entirely were the personal stories. Sometimes he'd spend the whole programme just talking to the women of Ireland with all their problems and no problem was too big or too small. He would get down to the level of the person he was talking to. He would listen, really listen. He would never trip over a person. He'd let them have their say.'

Dad was a performer at heart – an entertainer following the likes of Eamonn Andrews, who had inspired him as a young presenter and whose career he wished to emulate. He was a perfectionist, too. Billy Wall remembers Gay coming in early to the RTÉ radio centre every morning, going through that day's material and reading the letters aloud, rehearsing different accents and emphases.

Dad played the piano all the time at home. His playing was such a feature of our home life that we didn't really pay any heed. He always played upbeat, well-known jazz tunes with lots of chords, from what I can remember. He rarely played for people, with the exception of his friends from Donegal. In their homes, he would often play, accompanied by Paul Sweeney on trumpet, and they would all sing the same songs, and every time as if it was the first time. Always happy tunes, interspersed with lots of laughs. He continued to play right up until the chemotherapy treatment for his cancer rendered his fingertips numb.

One morning in 1977, Patrick Griffin was listening to *The Gay Byrne Hour*. Gay had announced a particular song but his producer played a joke on him, instead playing a recent recording of Gay playing jazz piano at a party. Inspired by the segment, Patrick wrote a poem and rushed to his local post office in Kilkenny. 'Next morning,' he said, 'Gay read my poem. No, he dramatised it and I have that recording. A treasured possession for all time. I will always hear it as Gay performed. "Gaybo's Piano Roll".'

```
Sing a few bars, everyone cried,
We'd love to hear an auld song.
Well now you're lucky, Gaybo replied,
For I've brought me piano along.
And to think that I nearly forgot it,
Sure, I wouldn't have brought it at all,
But tonight when I left for the party,
```

It was standing right there in the hall.
'Are you goin' to the party without me?
Do I have to get down on me knees?'
Asked the overstrung, upright piano
As he spoke through his ivory keys.
Well, me heart nearly broke as he stood there,
And I thought, 'Now what harm can I do
If I bring him along to the party
And play an auld medley or two?'
So, I pulled the piano behind me,
And I dragged it along up the street,
Though we got funny looks and strange glances,
From the people we happened to meet.
We finally got to the party,
And everything was in full swing,
And I knew it was worth all the effort,
When somebody asked me to sing.
'What a pity we don't have a piano,'
The drunk in the corner cried.
And I said, 'It's funny you should ask me,
'cos I happen to have one outside.'
So, they wheeled in the upright piano,
And I said, 'Now I'll play just for you.'
Someone cried 'Play some songs by Tchaikovsky',
And the drunk asked for *Rhapsody in Blue*.
So I started to finger the keyboard,
And everyone else sang along,
But two-and-a-half minutes later,
I came to the end of the song.
Then I closed the lid of the piano,
And somebody shouted 'encore'.
And I had to be truthful and tell them,
That I just couldn't play any more.

```
'Is that all?' they cried when I finished,
I said, 'That's the one song I play.'
So they said, 'Carry on. Play the same song again',
And I looked at them all in dismay.
But, they told me to go on and play it,
'Sure, we won't mind the same song at all,
For we can't tell what song you are playin',
When we're lyin' blind drunk in the hall.'
So, if you are asked to a party,
You're sure to be asked for a song,
Here's some advice that I'll give you,
Bring your piano along!
```

'I absolutely adored his programmes,' Catherine Corless said recently. 'We'd tune in just when the kids were going out to school ... You could potter around the kitchen and still do everything. Some bits you mightn't be that interested in – I wouldn't have been interested in politics at the time or anything like that – but that was Gay – he'd have absolutely everything and anything on the show.'

Gay's blend of music, chat and requests proved successful and, more important, a ratings hit. In 1979, in recognition of the show's increasing popularity, *The Gay Byrne Hour* was renamed *The Gay Byrne Show* and his scheduling slot expanded to two hours. The longer format meant that Gay could give time to more in-depth interviews while also maintaining the light-hearted element that was fundamental to the show. The bags of letters continued to arrive at the radio studio every week. As the years went by and *The Gay Byrne Show* tackled more controversial subjects, sparking conversations and playing an important role in lifting the lid on the nation's long-held secrets, the sense of fun and light relief that Gay and his team started out with was maintained.

Gay particularly liked letters that offered glimpses into quiet, private moments, such as this one:

```
Dear Gay,
Please do not read my address as it will give the game away
and cause a few red faces, as you will see. The other night,
```

as I sat in my car, I observed a garda and a bean garda patrol my area. As they passed a Chinese restaurant, they stopped and read the menu board. Then, lo and behold, his arm went around her waist and she his. They snuggled into each other and then separated and continued their patrol.

Did I just witness a magical moment in the life of a garda?

Is this a way to relieve the boredom of the night shift? Is this a public relations exercise to get recruits into the gardaí? What do you think, Gay? What do listeners think?

Actually, it softened my image of the gardaí.

Yours,

In 1985, an unusual phenomenon provoked hysteria across Ireland: moving statues. In July of that year, an observer in Ballinspittle, County Cork reported seeing a statue of the Virgin Mary moving spontaneously. Shortly afterwards, similar reports of moving statues were made in around 30 other locations. Like most other media outlets, Gay covered the phenomenon on his show. Today, the responses seem wonderfully innocent, but they are a good indication of just how religious the vast majority of the country was at this time.

Gay was talking there about moving statues and saying that they'd stopped moving ... He was sort of mocking the whole thing ... Now statues have been moving near me, but they haven't been recently. The reason for this is, I think, because Our Lady has come and given us a message that if we don't mend our ways, something terrible is going to happen in ten years. I believe that and I don't think she has to repeat this over and over ... She has come and given the message and her work is done.

According to this listener, it wasn't just the Virgin Mary who was appearing to the people of Ireland, but a whole cast of religious figures.

3/12/86

Dear Gay,

Please do not read my address as it will give the game away and cause a few red faces as you will see.

The other night as I sat in my car I observed a Garda and a ban Garda patrol my area. As they passed a chinese restaurant they stopped and read its menu board. Then low and behold his arm went around her waist and she his. They snuggled into each other and then separated and continued their patrol.

Did I just witness a magical moment in the life of a Garda? Is this a way to relieve the boredom of the night shift? Is this a public relations exercise to get recruits into the Garda?

What do you think gay?

What do listeners think?

Actually It softened my image of the Gardai.

Yours.

████████

> I went two weeks ago to Mount Melleray and I, along with
> my friends, saw the faces of the Sacred Heart and the old
> Pope John, and a nun … Maybe Saint Bernadette.

Even when the initial buzz died down, the sites acted as places of intrigue. People travelled from all over the country to visit them – it's believed that up to 100,000 people visited the Ballinspittle grotto alone. According to this listener, it doesn't matter that people moved on from the story – the important thing to remember is that the statues were moving in the first place:

> Asking why the statues are not moving is a pretty stupid
> question. Just because they are not being reported doesn't
> mean that they are not moving. I was down at the one in
> Ballinspittle and I saw it moving and there were plenty of
> people down there - not so many as in the first days of the
> moving statues, but a pretty constant flow. The media has
> lost interest in the whole thing but that doesn't mean that
> the statues have lost interest - or have stopped moving.

Crowds assembled at Ballinspittle.

Whatever news item was topical on any given day, Gay was sure to receive correspondence about it. On 8 February 1983, an armed gang stole the prize-winning thoroughbred racehorse Shergar from the Aga Khan's stud farm. In their investigation, Gardaí limited the information that was released to the press. As a result, the media began to speculate on what happened to Shergar, and the coverage naturally caught the public's imagination. Speculation was rife and many hoaxes were played. Gay received this anonymous letter:

Dear Gay,

I was given information some time ago which might possibly throw light on the whereabouts and/or lead to the recovery of Shergar.

The source of my information I cannot disclose (I think the clairvoyant lady who was recently on TV might play a significant part in tracing Shergar).

If you think my information may be of any importance, I would be prepared to contact you personally and give you full details. I want no publicity and no mention of Shergar, but you might perhaps let me know somehow on your morning show, or on your Late Late Show, whether you are interested in further details. […]

I am only interested in Shergar's safety and in the hope that he is alive and unharmed. I feel sure that my source of information is fairly reliable.

I shall await with interest your reaction to my letter. I do not want to get involved and must therefore remain anonymous.

Signed,

'Someone interested in Shergar's welfare'

HE IS ALIVE A...
I FEEL SURE THAT MY
OF INFORMATION IS FA...
RELIABLE.

I SHAI,

PART IN TRACING SHERGAR).
IF YOU THINK MY INFO-
RMATION MAY BE OF ANY
IMPORTANCE, I WOULD BE PREPARED
TO CONTACT YOU PERSONALLY
AND GIVE YOU FULL DETAILS.
I WANT NO PUBLICITY AND NO
MENTION OF SHERGAR, BUT YOU
MIGHT PERHAPS LET ME KNOW
SOMEHOW ON YOUR MORNING
SHOW, OR ON YOUR LATE LATE
SHOW, WHETHER YOU ARE
INTERESTED IN FURTHER
DETAILS.

There was no shortage of the varied content that could be sent to Gay. Whatever mattered to his listeners mattered to him. Reading the letters in the archive today is fascinating because, on the surface, the letters may purport to be about one particular issue, but they also reveal much about the social and cultural context of the time: the mid-eighties saw the emergence of the HIV virus and what would become the AIDS epidemic. On its surface, this letter from a member of the Gardaí is light-hearted and humorous, if a little stomach-churning.

Dear Gay,

I just finished a week of night duty. During the week we had to go to a certain licensed premises at three o'clock in the morning because an alarm was going. In the course of searching the pub for intruders, I went down into the cellar with the barman, who happened to be the keyholder. As you know, the cellar is the engine room of a public house. It's where all the barrels are tapped, with the supply lines going up to the top in the bar [or] lounge, as the case may be.

Beside the barrels, I saw two buckets of liquid. One appeared to be stout and the other lager or ale. I asked the barman what they were and he said they were slop; that is, leftovers and the drains of unfinished pints, all poured into the buckets. I asked him what they did with them and he just looked at me and grinned and said: 'Ah, I couldn't be telling you that!'

The whole world and its mother knows that publicans, in order to increase profit margins, put the slops back into the barrel to be served up to unsuspecting customers. Some publicans will tell you that they can send back bad barrels to Guinness and get a discount for them. The point of my letter is this:

With the current publicity that AIDS, hepatitis and its transmission is getting, is it possible that unscrupulous publicans are helping the spread of AIDS and hepatitis by pouring back into the slops, which may have been the remnants of some carrier's pint, who had slurped and slobbered over his last pint?

I know there are lots of women who are married to men who are proud to boast that they are 'ten-pints-a-night' men, and I know that with the abuse some of these women get from drunken husbands, they would be delighted if their husbands got AIDS, hepatitis, herpes, ulcers, blood pressure and every other ailment going.

Or, if they just blew up sitting on their high stools at the bar, so much the better. But what about all us moderate drinkers? Do we have to endure the prospect of getting AIDS or hepatitis just because an unscrupulous publican puts the slops (with the saliva and spittle included) back into the barrel, just to make a fast buck?

Sincerely,

This is a relatively light letter but one which sparked a furore for weeks afterwards, with many letters to Gay and heated defence from publicans. What was amusing in the letter and the outrage that followed was the horror that people focused on – publicans serving slops – rather than any possible disease transmission.

Pubs have always been great sources for news and stories. Just as in real life, pubs also featured in the correspondence that Gay received. In a letter written to Gay in 1979, Carmel McCartney told him of the discrimination against women in Ireland's public houses. In Carmel's letter, she explains that she was a new mum who was looking forward to a night out in her local pub in Inchicore, Dublin. When she got to the bar, she asked for a pint and was told by the barman that they didn't serve pints to ladies – she would have to make do with glasses of beer. As such, this meant that women were paying more money for their beer, as two glasses were more expensive than one pint. Gay took up the cause and debated the issue on air with the pub's owners. Not long after, the pub changed its policy, and Carmel, and other women, could sit back and enjoy their much-deserved full pints.

This story of 'pint equality' is one of the earliest examples of how the letters written to Gay could effect real social change. This period in the show, from 1973 to the early 1980s, would see the key relationship between Gay and his listeners being built and reinforced. Here was someone who they knew would take their queries, concerns, stories and problems seriously – no matter how frivolous or important. *The Gay Byrne Show* would continue in this way – light entertainment, jokes, on-air proposals, Local Hero nominations and mystery sound competitions – throughout much of its 25-year run. But just as Carmel McCartney had learned that Gay was listening and could pick up a cause, his other listeners had realised the same thing.

Over the years, the reaction to the female-focused content of the radio show wasn't always positive. Later, Gay reflected that negative reactions to the material often came from Irish women themselves, who sometimes felt threatened by conversations around feminism, independence and inequality. Many didn't want to upset the status quo that they had known all their lives.

In 1988 Gay received this letter, from an irate (presumably male) writer ...

Dear Sir,

I am absolutely convinced, without any doubt, that Mr/Ms Gay Byrne, in my opinion, thinks he's actually changing from a man into a woman.

I've noticed this in the last six months or so, particularly listening to him on his radio show. For example, what sane man, unless he had the intention of a sex change, would listen to, day after day, women on the phone to him about ladies' corsets, the royal family, childbirth, romance stories, women's underwear, women's rights, sex, etc., and 'isn't he gorgeous?'. Everything and anything related to women - he just loves it.

I say again - there's no sane man could put up with it, unless he was going for the change.

I think it's time to get a bit of culture and sanity back on RTÉ Radio 1.

Although the show appealed to a wide audience, both male and female, the men of Ireland were not really listening to what was afoot. Over the early years of the show, Gay's predominantly female audience had realised that he could provide a platform on which they could speak about what was important to them. Not only that, but they knew that a community of eager listeners had gathered, who had demonstrated that they were there to offer advice, encourage and support. They started to write in their droves.

2

The Nation's Confidant

—

A winter's morning, early 1980s. 7.45 am. In 90 minutes, *The Gay Byrne Show* will go live in studio 5. Gay's desk is neatly laid with his running order, research briefs, newspaper cuttings and music list. He is speaking animatedly to a dead microphone, oblivious to the presence and bustle of producers, researchers, secretaries and engineers. He rehearses aloud a listener's letter, pauses to make a note on the page: 'Insert laugh and comment'. Starts again. His voice is warm; then cools, for contrast. His face livens for emphasis. Now his tone changes: he has the measure of the story. Like a good actor with a script, as he speaks the words, he has found the meaning and the depth of the emotions involved. He's confident now that, live on air, he will do justice to the writer, and to the listener. He pauses. Then: next letter.

John Caden, Producer, *The Gay Byrne Show*, 1979-1986

John Caden worked with Gay as a researcher on *The Late Late Show* prior to producing his radio show. The years in which Caden was producer (1979–1986) were some of the most important for the show – a time of significant social change in Ireland, which Gay and the show bore witness to.

In many ways, John and Gay were opposites. John's politics were aligned to the left and Gay was a conservative. But Gay believed that they met somewhere in the middle, and that the programme was improved for it. They worked incredibly well together and Gay's respect for John was well known. He said of John: 'A presenter in a studio feels secure when John is outside in the control room.' As the show's new producer, John wanted to take a more socially aware approach, and this, with Gay's unique instinct for what his audience wanted to hear, would successfully change the direction of the programme.

CHEERS . . . Gay celebrates with producer John Cadden after the final radio show of the season.

As Ireland was busy congratulating itself on its upstanding, devout citizens and way of life, Gay was hearing a different story. People who did not yet feel brave enough to speak openly on the many injustices and problems they were living with every day were now given the opportunity to share their struggles with Gay. They knew that whatever they shared, he would treat them with respect and empathy. He was the person to whom they could turn when they had nobody else to speak to – not even, or sometimes especially not, their closest family and friends.

While the light and heart-warming letters continued to arrive, letters hinting at darker secrets began to trickle in. These letters spoke of uncomfortable truths, that all was not what it seemed from the outside. These letters spoke of harsh Catholic upbringings and education, disapproving social judgements, the powerlessness of poverty, unhappy marriages and hidden personal secrets.

Billy Wall remembers one of the earliest of this type of letter, which came in during the mid-seventies. 'We got a letter from an "unmarried mother". Nothing like that was ever broadcast before – it was so strange. With some trepidation, we decided that we would broadcast it. This lady was looking for accommodation and didn't have anywhere to live. We got five or six offers from people who would gladly help her out. And that was the beginning of what followed in the years after that.' RTÉ management was wary of Gay venturing into this sort of territory and Billy admits that, at the time, the radio team retreated, for a time, back to the default of light-hearted, happy content.

When we look back now at *The Gay Byrne Show* and the thousands of letters that were sent to Gay, it might be easy to think that he had free rein to discuss anything and everything on the show, but behind the scenes there was a string of hard-fought battles. Gay himself alluded to these on occasion, but to properly understand the context of many of these letters, it is important to consider the power of the Church, the State and the many people who, at the time, weren't going to let their control be loosened. The power of the Church and the State was absolute and all-encompassing. John Caden said, 'The weekly meetings of the RTÉ editorial board, chaired by the director-general, waded through mountains of news cuttings and letters of complaint from ministers, TDs, councillors, bishops, priests, and "influential" Catholics.'

But since Gay's listenership figures were soaring – and, with them, advertising revenue – there was little RTÉ programme controllers could do to stop the show, despite pushback from the Church and various professional bodies. Recently, when asked why Gay gave so much time to the letters, John responded, 'It was box office.'

While many people felt isolated or without support, sharing their experiences showed that there were many others out there just like them. As the letters continued to arrive, momentum continued to build until people were forced to sit up and listen. And Gay wanted to make sure that these people would have their voices heard.

Many letters like this one revealed the hidden horrors in Irish society.

> Dear Gay,
>
> On reading the sad case of […] and the 11-year-old girl whose mother was supposedly downstairs. I am a mother myself now in my 50s. When I was four years old, I had a similar experience, only it was my own father. My mother was also downstairs.
>
> I was pinned down on the bed by a big man (my father), pulling at my clothes, pinching and pulling at my flesh. I remember everything. I screamed like an animal, screeching, wailing for my mother who was only downstairs. I remember my father's eyes, his laughing, his mouth, him hurting me. Unless my mother dropped dead, she could not but have heard me. But my mother, when I eventually ran to her, could not face me or look at me, don't mind comfort me. It still pains me today to think of the disappointment of the lack of support I got. I grew up that day at four years of age. I avoided my father - always putting up with his exposing himself throughout the years of growing up. He is dead now, but he damaged me for life. But I managed to protect my own daughters who are now in their twenties […]
>
> I have harboured this secret all my life alone.

Looking back today, it is so difficult to fully understand the incredible injustices and restrictions endured by women, and the disregard for their basic rights. These were the mothers and grandmothers of my own peer group. This was not that long ago. Women were often powerless within their marriages, with very few rights and laws with which to protect themselves. Marriage and married life were often discussed on the show, and Gay received many letters describing loved-up tales of happy marriages. The show even ran a 'Perfect Partner' segment around Valentine's Day – but there was also a significant proportion detailing unhappy marriages.

Dear Lyay

On reading this sad case of ██████████ and the 11 year old girl whose mother was supposedly downstairs. I am a mother myself now in my 50s. When I was four years old, I had a similar experience, only it was my own father. My mother was also downstairs.

I was pinned down on the bed by a big man (my father), pulling at my clothes, pinching and pulling at my flesh. I remember everything. I screamed like an animal, screeching, wailing for my mother who was only downstairs. I remember my father's eyes, his laughing, his mouth, him hurting me. Unless my mother dropped dead, she could not but have heard me. But my mother, when I eventually ran to her, could not face me or look at me,

Maureen and Gay in later years.

Psychologist and broadcaster Dr Maureen Gaffney was a regular contributor to *The Gay Byrne Show*. In an Ireland where mental health issues were brushed under the carpet and in which psychology was a new phenomenon, Dr Gaffney would respond to phone-in questions from the audience, in the process becoming one of Ireland's most respected voices in her field. She was regularly asked for advice on marriage and home life. This letter references a guest slot in which she appeared, while also sharing a very private family tragedy.

Dear Gay,

Perhaps Maureen might comment some day on the effects of tragedy on a good marriage. Personally, I would have thought that it would bring a couple closer together, but now I know differently.

We married in our very early twenties. We had little […] and my husband had a secure if lowly paid job. Over the following 16 years we built a family and a house and garden, which we did with our own hands. We were a very happy family. My husband was a gentle, loving, good-natured man, and we lived for one another and the kids. We had two major events every year, Christmas and our summer holidays. We saved half a year for each and we had some wonderful times. Our kids saw every corner of this island, from the back of an old Bedford van into which we piled them and a tent every summer and headed off for two weeks. We had our share of ups and downs. I lost the second of my parents; he lost his mother and a sister. But we were always there for one another and we carried on.

Then, out of a clear blue sky, our middle boy came down with a serious illness, and in one week we had lost him. The whole family was shattered. I don't have to go into the details. You are well aware of the weeks following such an event. As the weeks passed, however, it became apparent that Daddy was slowly crawling into a shell and closing it behind him. He spent all his spare time in bed, he spoke to no one and he hated to hear anyone laugh or be funny or happy in the house.

I had children who needed to be loved, fed and generally taken care of, but I found myself completely on my own. He simply did not want to know. I tried to get him to talk to me. I remember waking one night at 2 a.m., finding him not in the bed. I went to the living room and there he was sitting, smoking. I knelt on the floor in front of him and begged him to talk to me, to hold me and that we might comfort one another. I'll never forget how he pushed me away. He could not take me inside his grief. He kept saying, 'I can't help it. My life is over.' I even suggested that we go to a counsellor, but he would not hear of that! All this time (two-three years), people had great sympathy for him: 'He's taking it so badly, and you are great, you're so strong.' This used to kill me. No one only the older children seemed to realise that my heart was broken in two and the pain was even greater because I had no one to share it with. I think that for part of that time I nearly hated my husband for abandoning me. It sounds dreadful, but if I'm honest, I think it is true.

Ten years further on, and life has settled again for us. Our children are almost grown, and better young people you would not meet anywhere. They never gave us a minute's trouble. We have had many occasions to be proud of them, thankfully. My husband has settled back into himself, thank God, but he is a changed person. He is still loving and kind, but he sees the world now through a grey-tinted window. He never looks forward with anticipation to anything. He is very slow to show real joy in any of the children's achievements. It's as if he must protect himself from hurt.

I have changed, too, I've no doubt. Maybe I'm stronger, although I don't think so. I can't bear to hear sad stories of other people's troubles, although I can help them in a personal way - when I steel myself to go forward and do so. We have a quiet house as the young people are moving on and we must get used to that. We are happy and contented in one another's company, but I feel that the joy has gone from our lives. Perhaps in time we will be able to re-kindle it again.

The point of this long piece is that I now know there is no such thing as an indestructible marriage. It is a very delicate flower, very easily destroyed.

As a new decade began, the 1980s in Ireland was a difficult time for many. Unemployment was rife – Ireland's labour market was one of the worst performers in Europe, with the unemployment rate rising to 17 per cent by 1986. Unemployment and emigration form the foundation for so many issues within families and homes, as reflected in the letters in this book. Marital problems, alcohol abuse, poverty and so many other issues have unemployment as their root cause. Unemployment is a prevalent theme in so many of the letters included here, whether or not they are directly about the issue, and they show just how widespread unemployment was in Ireland at the time. It was part and parcel of Irish life.

Despite unemployment being so common, many of the letters speak about the shame of it: the indignity of drawing the dole and trying to live on these small payments, parents not being able to buy their children new clothes or presents, and the stigma they struggled with in school when faced with other children who were better off. Unemployment is not just demoralising for the people directly affected, it can also be difficult for close family members to watch, too. This letter, written by a 15-year-old schoolgirl, shares her experience of

Dear Gay

I am fifteen years old and I listen
to your programme as I am on my mid term
break and I would like to air my veiws on
your programme. I don't know if other young
people would share the same point of veiws as I.
My father works five days a week and loves
His job I suppose you could class him as a work-
acholic. The money he gets is very small comparison
to what he use to get years ago. We had a better stan
-ard of living then. Yet if he complains to his boss
he is told that there are thousands of people that
would love his job. This man had other people working
for him but they left and went on the doel because
they were getting less money for working and more
money on the doel. Before my father got this job, he
was two years unemployed and he hated being on the
doel. My father loves he trade and realy enjoys
working. I think it is unfair that people are
being treated like this. My father and mother tried
to emigrate to Austraila and Canada but were turned
down I suppose it was because we had no relations away
My mother and father both want the best for us like
most good parents would. I see now most couples are
getting separated due to financial presure on them,
It is very hard on couples now that christmas is coming
up. I see my parents under alot of pressure as
I have two young brothers who are looking forward to 'Santy'
coming and my parents are very worried if they'll be able
to afford 'Santy'. My mother is praying for a mircle. I
feel that the Governement is not only running the
people out of this country but also with the financial press-
-ure on the parents, are trying to break families up. or may-be
they dont realize it because they themselves are not under

watching others suffer from unemployment, while also contending with the fact that, due to her family's reduced income, her own prospects for the future may become limited.

'It is salutary to remember, in these hard times,' Gay said, as he read out the letter, 'that it is perhaps often harder for people watching others suffering, through lack of money, or a job, than for the people going directly through the experience, like a family member ... I think this young girl ... has put down very strongly, yet simply, just what it is like for families to grow up, wondering, watching parents cope, hoping, yet knowing that miracles aren't on.'

I am 15 years old and I listen to your programme as I am on my mid-term break and I would like to air my views on your programme. I don't know if other young people would share the same point of view as I.

My father works five days a week and loves his job. I suppose you could class him as a workaholic. The money he gets is very small compared to what he used to get years ago. We had a better standard of living then. Yet, if he complains to his boss, he is told that there are thousands of people that would love his job. This man had other people working for him but they left and went on the dole because they were getting less money for working and more money on the dole. Before my father got this job, he was two years unemployed and he hated being on the dole. My father loves his trade and really enjoys working. I think it is unfair that people are being treated like this. My father and mother tried to emigrate to Australia and Canada but were turned down. I suppose it was because we had no relatives away.

My mother and father both want the best for us, like most good parents would. I see now most couples are getting separated due to financial pressure on them. It is very hard on couples now that Christmas is coming up. I see my parents under a lot of pressure as I have two young brothers who are looking forward to Santy coming and my parents are very worried if they'll be able to afford 'Santy'. My mother is praying for a miracle. I feel that the government is not only running the people out of this country but also, with the financial pressure on the parents, are trying to break families up, or maybe they don't realise it because they themselves are not under financial pressure.

I myself would like to go to third-level education and would love to get on in life, please God. But I can't see that happening, unless my parents get a little miracle. I suppose there are thousands of young people like me who want to do well and go to third-level education but their families are not in a position to give it to them. I think this is very sad.

Throughout the show's run, it was important to Gay that he should air as many differing views on a particular subject as possible. He always maintained that it was not his job to push one agenda over another. In many ways, he acted as a thermometer for the zeitgeist – taking the temperature of social issues and presenting complex, often contradictory, opinions on them. It was not his intention always to provoke reactions; rather, he wanted to present as clear a picture as possible. A community can feature many points of view, and his community of listeners was no different. Unemployment was one such issue. When Gay read out certain letters describing people's experiences, he would, in turn, receive letters from others who criticised people on social welfare payments, or who offered suggestions that weren't always appreciated. Take this letter as an example.

Dear Gay,

In answer to the Clontarf woman who knows where there's plenty of work, please send her my name and address and I will write away. I will also send on the addresses of all my friends who have left the country to seek employment.

Can this woman honestly say there's plenty of work if I just get up and look? Why? When did she last look? Or, indeed, when has she been last at an interview?

Only last night, Gay, I cried myself to sleep as I'm now entering my fifth month roaming around. Every day I apply for work.

I get £45 per week and spend a large amount on stationery, photocopies and photographs. If I answer box numbers, I walk to town and drop them in by hand. I don't have a telephone, so I'm hard to contact by agencies.

I'm 23. I've had a string of badly paid temporary positions. I've sold footwear, hardware, fabric, groceries. I've worked as a clerical assistant, receptionist, telephonist, secretary and sandwich maker.

Thank you for your time, Gay. Your voice has filled my room each morning for the last number of months. Without it, I would be very lonely.

The next letter describes the shame that so many people were forced to feel, through no fault of their own, due to unemployment. In so many of these letters, what's striking is that those who are fighting poverty are not looking for material things. They are hard-working, decent people who simply want the dignity of work so that they can pay basic bills and provide for their children – a universal experience.

The Gay Byrne Show

(Type)

R TE.

Dublin.

Dear Gay.

Re your correspondant the lady who criticised the unemployed galway man for feeling sorry for himself. I would make the following points.

The lady critic completly missed the point. All the work she outlines is ~~completly~~ of great value in itself both to the country and the person who does it personally. To do this would certainly ease the mans mind and make him feel more usefull. and wanted by society, However it can never replace the feeling of utter uselesness which any man feels when he realizes that he can never again "earn his bread by the sweat of his brow" As I have known both sides of this story.

No satisfaction gained by the teaching of an illiterate child or raising money for somalia can replace the utter desolation you feel when you cannot through no fault of your own give for example your children money for a school trip or even pay the E.SB Bill. which you cannot do on the dole money,

To say otherwise is like saying that you can get drunk by passing Guinnesses Brewery and shows the complete lack of understanding of unemployment which in fact.

P/To

Dear Gay,

Re your correspondent - the lady who criticised the unemployed man for feeling sorry for himself - I would make the following points:

The lady critic completely missed the point. All the work she outlines is of great value in itself both to the country and the person who does it personally. To do this would certainly ease the man's mind and make him feel more useful and wanted by society. However, it can never replace the feeling of utter uselessness which any man feels when he realises that he can never again 'earn his bread by the sweat of his brow', as I have known both sides of this story.

No satisfaction gained by the teaching of an illiterate child or raising money for Somalia can replace the utter desolation you feel when you cannot, through no fault of your own, give, for example, your children money for a school trip or even pay the ESB bill, which you cannot do on the dole money.

To say otherwise is like saying that you can get drunk by passing Guinness's brewery and shows the complete lack of understanding of unemployment, which in fact causes it to be such a tragedy to those unemployed.

Yours,

This letter offers yet another point of view on unemployment — or, rather, employment. The economic depression experienced in Ireland during the 1980s meant that self-employed people also struggled to make ends meet.

Dear Gay,

Yesterday was my 20th wedding anniversary. There was no card, no flowers or no meal out this year. You see, Gay, we are self-employed, not unemployed, and we owe a lot of money. My husband works awfully hard but the more he works the more it costs, and we just never seem to get ahead of ourselves. The bills just seem to get bigger. All our money goes into the business.

Sometimes, I get so annoyed when I hear about the unemployed and how hard up they are. Well, let me tell you, I would gladly swap with some of the unemployed. They are the ones who get everything free. We, the self-employed, get nothing.

We never used to want for anything but, at the present time, I am feeding two adults and four children on £70 and less per week. There seems to be no light at the end of the tunnel. It is so hard to go from having plenty to wanting for everything and know that unless I was to get £5,000, I will never get out of this terrible trouble I am in. I pray and pray to win some money, but God never seems to hear my prayer.

I seem to never stop crying and the depression that I feel is unbearable, day and night. I hide all this from my husband because I know how upset he is, so I keep up for his sake. We both put on a brave face for family and friends. Who wants to know anyway?

Have a very happy, peaceful and prosperous Christmas and New Year.

God bless you all.

With high unemployment came high levels of emigration, with many people feeling they had no option but to leave Ireland in search of a brighter future. During the severe economic recession in the first half of the 1980s, a 'migration culture' developed in Ireland. Large swathes of the population moved abroad, especially to the United States, for better job opportunities and a higher quality of life. It is estimated that, during the 1980s, about one in seven left Ireland, both individuals and families, and travelled to America to start a new life. The heartbreak evident in written communications to Gay took many forms – in addition to the letters, many poems, drawings and photos can be found in the archives today. Different people find different ways of expressing themselves. This person was inspired to write a poem to communicate how they felt about the widespread emigration that touched the lives of so many people at this time.

```
I did not weep when she said she would go, pretending
it was best for her
But at the airport, watching her disappear, the pain
was unbelievable
Would I be able to stay the pace?
I chided myself with health, husband, home - but, oh,
the empty place at the table!
The days were a lasting of Gethsemane until the first
phone call.
'Mammy, I've got digs and a job. It's not bad at all
And I know it will get better. I'll write a letter
every week
To say how I get on. When I ring, speak of home,
neighbours and friends.'
Yes, love, I will speak of everything you want to hear
but never the pain of parting
Tears I shed every night I lay down my head, to
remember your
Birthing, rearing, going away
The way I feel
Nor the price I paid for the package deal.
```

Despite the decimating effect of emigration on families, the lure of the US in particular was compelling, as is clearly shown by the following letter.

Dear Gay,

In the light of recent discussions on your programme regarding emigration, I thought you might be interested to hear of my own family's story.

Four years ago, there were 11 members of my family, including my father and my mother, living in Ireland. Today, there are only three of us left - the rest have emigrated to America.

My older brother could see no future here. He now lives in New York, where he has married and they have a thriving business there.

My younger brother could see no future prospects here. He's a barman now, and his wife a waitress. They have saved $10,000 between them since they emigrated under two years ago. They would never have saved that here in such a short time.

My father emigrated in July of this year and my mother and another brother and sister joined him in September. In his first two months there, my father had saved $1,000, which was a fortune to him.

Another sister emigrated with her baby in October because she wanted her child to have a better future. She's very happily settled now and maintaining herself and her child. She can even envisage relaxed relationships with men, which would otherwise have been frowned upon in this very religious though not always very Christian country of ours.

The only sad ending to any of the above stories was the sudden death of my father. Naturally, we all mourn the death of a man who raised us all as a closely knit family and who paved the way for all of us with sound advice and guidance, but we all know that his last three months on earth were his happiest.

My mother, now a widow with two young children to support, is remaining in America where we buried my father. She is now living in a country which offers her plenty of work to support the younger members of the family. She has a better chance at a new lease of life than she would ever have in her native country.

In the short time I spent in America, at my father's funeral, I grew to love the country. It is alive and vibrant, and I would love to live there. My husband has a good secure job and my children will never have to do without the essentials in life, so it is not necessary for us to emigrate in the financial sense.

I have been unable to get employment … for nearly three years now, but I realise that I am fortunate to have at least one wage earner in our household. It does not, however, justify the lack of employment available.

People may speak of the crime rate in other countries but in the light of recent murders and child disappearances, are we in this country far behind? I am personally living in an area where the Northern conflict is only a few miles away and said conflict often spills over into this country, and every day I wonder how long more peace will prevail in the South?

My point is, Gay, that anyone who has the opportunity and the will and wish to emigrate should do so, be they young or old. All my family love Ireland but those who have emigrated have no wish to return permanently. The grass may not always be greener on the other side of the mountain, but you may as well see it first and find out.

Yours sincerely,

While *The Gay Byrne Show* never lost its sense of fun, and light-hearted, nostalgic segments still featured heavily on the show, the beginning of the 1980s – and the social, economic and political problems that dominated that decade – saw a different type of letter arrive at the RTÉ radio centre. Gay had worked hard to develop a level of trust with his listeners. Slowly, the letters began to lift the veil on many harsh and uncomfortable truths about Ireland – truths that people had known and endured for a long time. These long-held secrets had been bubbling under the surface for some time. Now, supported by one another, people were emboldened to share their secrets with Gay. Ireland would spend the following decades, right up to the present day, grappling with and unravelling what was about to be revealed.

3

Behind Closed Doors

—

THROUGHOUT THE 1970S AND 1980S, it was widely accepted that young Irish women would find a suitable partner, get married, and carry out their expected duties of having children, caring for an expanding family and tending to the home. Happy marriages were regularly celebrated on the show, and Gay facilitated a number of on-air proposals during the show's run.

In 1986, Irene Bloomer wrote to Gay to nominate her husband, Stan, for a fun 'Perfect Partner' segment. On Valentine's Day, on air, Irene recounts to Gay the romantic story of how Stan proposed to her, on Killiney Hill, and how they're still very much in love. Listening to the audio clip today, it's easy to hear Gay's natural warmth with women – he manages to both gently tease them while, at the same time, taking them seriously and really listening to them. They feel completely at ease with him, comfortable enough to share these private moments from their lives. Looking back on the segment, Stan now says of Gay: 'For a lot of people, he just was so safe to talk to. You felt he had this open heart and that you were only talking to him. But yet again, you weren't – you were talking to half a million, however many people were actually listening to the radio, and he was able to bring out of people what they really wanted to say, to get it off their chests and it was a safe environment.' The safe environment that Gay created allowed him to hear another side of the story.

Women's rights in Ireland were severely restricted in the 1970s and into the 1980s, especially when it came to marriage. Ireland's marriage bar was still in effect when Gay first came on air in 1973. Although the ban was abolished that year, in practice it would be many years before real change was effected. Divorce was not an option – and legislation allowing the dissolution of marriages would not be signed into law for another 23 years, in 1996. Couples whose marriage had broken down had very few options available to them, and many felt compelled to stay together, often in terrible circumstances.

Of course, things did not necessarily improve if a woman stayed in her marriage. Until 1974, the children's allowance, paid by the State, was paid directly to the father, unless he allowed his wife to collect the money. And until 1976, with the introduction of the Family Home Protection Act, a woman had no right to the home she shared with her husband, and he could sell it without her consent. If a woman suffered physical abuse at the hands of her husband, there was no legislation to have the man removed from the family home. Legislation enabling barring orders was introduced in 1976, but the order could only be for a maximum of three months and it was not widely enforced. It would not be until 1981 that it was increased to twelve months. Furthermore, under common law, a husband could not be found guilty of raping his wife. The notion of consent was a long way off and it was widely accepted that a man had the right to have sex with his wife whenever he wanted. Marital rape was not defined until 1990. There were certainly men who found themselves in difficult situations, but the people who suffered most frequently were women and children. Single 'deserted' mothers were often marginalised alongside 'unmarried mothers' in communities, and many struggled on in abusive marriages for financial reasons or so as not to offend or embarrass family members.

From the safety – or, in many cases, the unsafety – of their homes, these women began to write from the heart, opening up and spilling their darkest secrets to Gay. Thousands of heartbreaking letters sit in the RTÉ archives today: letters describing loveless marriages; physical and sexual abuse; absent husbands and fathers; alcoholic, violent men; financial control; as well as bullying, unsympathetic in-laws. What's striking about these letters is that, despite their dangerous situations, many of these women trusted Gay enough to enclose their names and addresses. Often, they requested Gay not to read out their name on air, and identifying information was always blacked out ahead of each show to avoid accidentally revealing it. Gay's research team would go through these letters painstakingly. They would type out each letter to be read on air and put it with the original, ensuring that no possible error in revealing an identity could arise. But it's telling that the women who wrote in trusted Gay with this information – they wanted him to know, to believe and to acknowledge them.

Gay speaks with listeners on Grafton Street during the 1988 *Gay Byrne Christmas Special.*

If a marriage broke down and the woman was left alone, often she wasn't allowed or able to return to work. Many found themselves unqualified for work in the first place, having left education early and married young. Others simply couldn't work due to the responsibility of rearing their children. Even if a woman did manage to find work, the pay she received was, on average, half that of a man's, before equal pay legislation was introduced in 1974 (and, even then, equal pay legislation did not in any way mean equal pay in reality).

The key to all these letters is not really the problems they expose but that for so long women had put up with these issues behind closed doors. It was this national outlet for people to speak out that was revolutionary. It was they who were the revolutionaries – Gay was simply their conduit.

The early trickle of letters about love and marriage were from an older generation, people in their fifties who had married in the 1950s and 1960s. These were the people in loveless, sexless marriages, due to the pressure and expectations of moralistic Catholic Ireland. Their letters chart upsetting stories of lost love, emotional neglect, miscommunication and overriding Catholic guilt.

This letter demonstrates the strict Catholic education with which most young Irish children at the time grew up. The full extent of the abuse in some schools that would come out in the following decades was not widely known, or, at least, publicly acknowledged, but this letter does describe a pervasive culture in which children and their needs and feelings were very often neglected.

I think we should remember that many people have gone through the Christian Brothers school system and have come out the other side as whole and fulfilled human beings. But a significant proportion of men have not and, in my experience, a significant majority of the sexually distressed men whom I see professionally have come through the Christian Brothers system. But that explanation is too simple. These difficulties usually originated in the home - often because no one demonstrated affection there. The parents did not show that they cared about each other. They did not touch each other, or their children. This resulted in feelings of very low self-worth, and people grew up having never experienced the feeling of being loved. Children from loving homes were usually very able to get through tough school systems more or less untarnished, but those who did not have that stabilising background tended to be badly damaged.

This letter-writer was determined to break the cycle of not demonstrating outward expressions of love or affection to children:

Dear Gay,
Why I'm writing? It's in reply to the woman who has an unresponsive husband. I was married to such a man […]. I thought I loved him. The more withdrawn he became, the more flamboyant I became. Sexual relations were almost non-existent: once during the last two years of our

marriage. We have one child. I thought that I could go on coping with this feeling of rejection, mainly because I had so many friends who loved me and made me <u>feel</u> loved. But I couldn't. Slowly but surely it was turning me into a hard and bitter person. Only <u>I</u> knew how bitter.

Then one day I saw my husband push our daughter away when she went to hug him. The hurt in her face nearly killed me. That very day, I packed a few suitcases and told him I was leaving and our child was coming with me. Well, Gay, I could see the hurt <u>and</u> the relief fighting for supremacy on his face. But we went. It hurt me, it really did, but no way could I see our daughter turn into another such as him, and I'm sure she must in such an atmosphere.

I've been separated now for three years. I never see him. I realise now that I didn't love him. It was pity I felt. I pitied him because I thought he <u>wanted</u> to make friends, wanted to be able to show emotion. But he didn't. He just wanted to be left alone. He is an emotional eunuch, if you like, and no one could change him.

I have men friends now, but I have not had sex with anyone, ever, other than my husband. All I ever wanted was to be held, hugged and to be shown affection. My daughter and I hug and kiss each other constantly. We don't have tuppence to rub together but we are far better off now than we ever were before.

I'm glad I made the break. My husband is content, too, I know, living with his inanimate objects that demand nothing from him.

I'm sorry this letter is so long. I tried to keep it short but if I wrote the whole story of how I felt, it would make *War and Peace* look puny.

Dear Gay,

Why I'm writing? It's in reply to the woman who has
an unresponsive husband. I was married to such a man
███████████. I thought I loved him. The more
withdrawn he became, the more flamboyant I became. Sexual
relations were almost non-existant; once during the last
2 years of our marriage. We have one child, ███████████
███. I thought that I could go on coping with this
feeling of rejection, mainly because I had so many friends
who loved me and made me _feel_ loved. But I couldn't.
Slowly but surely it was turning me into a hard and
bitter person. Only _I_ knew how bitter.

Then one day I saw my husband push our daughter away
when she went to hug him. The hurt in her face nearly
killed me. That very day, I packed a few suit-cases
and told him I was leaving and our child was coming with
me. Well Gay, I could see the hurt _and_ the relief
fighting for supremacy on his face. But we went. It
hurt me, it really did, but no way could I see our
daughter turn into another such as him, and I'm sure she
must in such an atmosphere.

I've been separated now for three years. I never see him.
I realise now that I didn't love him. It was pity I felt.
I pitied him because I thought he _wanted_ to make friends,
wanted to be able to show emotion. But he didn't. He just
wanted to be left alone. He is an emotional eunoch if
you like, and no one could change him.

I have men friends now, but I have not had sex with
anyone, ever, other than my husband. All I ever wanted
was to be held, hugged and to be shown affection. My daughter
and I hug and kiss each other constantly. We don't have
tuppence to rub together but we are far better off now
than we wexe ever were before.

The following letter is from a man whose marriage has never been consummated. It makes clear the deep-rooted and far-reaching influence of the Catholic Church's teaching on so many in Ireland.

In relation to your correspondence recently, over the past week, my wife and I have been married for over twenty years and our marriage has never been consummated. My wife has gone through a great deal of agony over this and it's something she is extremely reluctant to talk about. From the beginning she was extremely shy about everything to do with the Marriage Act. She's a warm, loving, gentle, sensitive and much-loved woman by her friends and neighbours. She has much love to give, except she cannot express it sexually. After about seven years of marriage, I talked her into going to see someone. The psychiatrists told us that it was not that uncommon in Ireland, and the major factor was 'harsh moral upbringing' in the younger years. My wife told him that sex had always been portrayed as something vulgar and vile, and not to be indulged in by the manners of the day. Although she was able eventually to get over her repulsion and fear of sex, she remained unable to have physical relations. I think her greatest pain was that she was not able to have children of our own. We did adopt children, and she has been the best mother in the world to them. They are almost healthy adults by now. Sometimes, when I realise the damage that was done to my wife in her youth, I do become disturbed by it. She is the most caring and loving woman in the world, and I wouldn't think of leaving her in a millennium. I must say we're both very careful about the upbringing of our children. We taught them that a loving sexual expression is healthy, wholesome and beautiful. Perhaps it's time we started thinking, talking and teaching about loving sex in this country, which it would seem is not necessarily always the same as legal sex.

The pain my wife's condition has caused both of us can never be uttered. It's beyond measure. I have watched her grief, unable to help her. You may well ask if I have ever been unfaithful to her? The answer is sometimes, but as far as I'm concerned, that's a non-issue. I've also been celibate for long, long periods in my life, as has been my wife all her life. I think, as a nation, we all have a lot of rethinking to do on the question of what sexual attitudes we give to our young people. I hope you read out this letter, so that maybe the extent of this problem may surface. 'Harsh moral upbringing' was the dominating factor in all our youths, and yet the extent of the damage remains unknown. Many choose to bear their cross in silence because it's been a subject that has never been raised. That is until you took the bull by the horns and have had the courage to take it on. I think it's time to bring this out of the closet. I know the high costs and pain and deprivation this beautiful woman and I have endured.

I did not mean to write such a long letter. But the deep, deep unspoken pain of all those years drove me onwards.

In the same vein, a letter from a young woman hints at a difficult childhood as a reason why she cannot bring herself to have sex with her husband.

Dear Gay,
I am a very young married woman (24). I love my husband very much, but rarely do I have any desire to make love.

I can't help this and really wish I could. Sometimes I can pretend, but is this unfair to my husband? I dread the day he might turn to another woman. He does love me very much, but how can I expect this to last? That woman's husband is probably going through hell, just like I am. We love our partners, but are unable to express this love.

A bad experience as a child may have left me like this. I can't be sure. Maybe if that woman dug deep into her husband's past, she'll find something there, that he has hidden away.

The letters written about loveless marriages, and their related topics, are difficult to read. Of course, they were even more difficult to live through and write about. But sharing these stories gave listeners some hope – that, despite what they had gone through in the past, their collective energy and refusal to accept the status quo meant that, finally, Ireland was beginning to free itself from the shackles of its 'harsh moral upbringing'. As with many of the subjects that Gay tackled on his programme, one letter could act as a springboard. Within days, *The Gay Byrne Show* could be flooded with letters in response from listeners all over Ireland who were in similar situations. It must be remembered that this was an Ireland where these things 'didn't happen', at least outwardly, and where there were few counsellors and even fewer supports for married couples. The Catholic Marriage Advisory Bureau and other church agencies, whose sole purpose was to encourage couples to stay together, were often the only option. Many couples outwardly lived happy, normal lives, but the reality behind closed doors was often very different. *The Gay Byrne Show* created a space where people could tell their stories anonymously to the nation – and lay bare the hidden misery behind many unions. In a later interview, Gay would describe the furious response in the early years to the mere mention of divorce or an impending discussion of divorce on either *The Gay Byrne Show* or *The Late Late Show*.

Marriage and family life continued to be a common theme throughout the run of *The Gay Byrne Show*. Even as women's rights improved over the decades, descriptions of family life often hinted at wider, interconnected issues – particularly around mental health and a judgemental society. This letter, received much later, in 1993, is on the surface about marriage, but it also alludes to loneliness, stigma and 'not letting the side down' – themes that imbue so many of the letters found in the archives.

Dear Gay,
The reason I am writing to you is firstly to give a piece of advice to anyone contemplating marriage and moving in with the in-laws.
    You see, Gay, I am living with my father-in-law, and to describe him as an ignorant pig would be understating

the matter. I cannot take any more of his behaviour. I am on the verge of a mental breakdown, and please don't say to tell him to move to one of my husband's family - it would be like showing a red rag to a bull.

He is impossible - my marriage cannot take the strain of it much longer, and I have two small children. My husband cannot talk to him and perhaps doesn't feel the strain the same way I do, as he is away much of the time. He knows how I feel but dares not open his mouth. We have tried getting our doctor to get round him, but he was abusive to him too.

The father-in-law is abusive to all his family, none of them can talk to him. His wife is dead. All I am asking for is for some time on my own with my husband and children. A few days - a week, if possible, on our own. We cannot go on holidays, either, as my husband is self-employed and right now is his busy time.

My husband's family would be angry if they knew that this problem was being aired. But they are not living constantly with him. They are away from him, and only have to put up with him for a few hours or a day, not weeks, months, years.

Please help. There is no one else who I can turn to. I feel so trapped. Please, please, let no young couple become caught like the way I have. I am sorry, Gay, I cannot write any more. I am crying silently to myself, and not even my husband has noticed me. Gay, today I am 32 years old. How long more must I live in hell? Thank you for reading this. If there is any advice which you can offer, I would be glad of it.

PS. I have to show the world that outwardly I am happy. Can't let the side down.

Dear Gay,

Thank you very much for broadcasting phone numbers of the Women's Aid refuge in Dublin on your morning show and I am very grateful to you for it. Yes, I am the mother of four children who was dazed on the floor and my children looking at me. You were shocked when reading it, but, Gay I could write a book of my life and it would be very ugly reading as it would contain very little happiness. I am not a bad housewife and mother but when you get repeated beatings, and most times you don't know what they were for, you begin to lose all confidence in yourself and you begin to believe it

own fault, and you
t. You stay away from
go into hiding until your
blue marks have faded.
tell you that when my
re smaller, I used to
hard to lift them out of
s I was all pains after
uld go on and on but
will say to you is thank
you for giving the phone numbers
If there are women out there
listening and are being beaten, or
abused in any way, use those
numbers and get out fast as it
won't stop but get worse.

Another letter, written in 1993, details some of the horrific abuse that the writer sustained at the hands of her husband over a prolonged period. She hopes that sharing her own story will empower someone else.

Dear Gay,

Thank you very much for broadcasting phone numbers of the Women's Aid refuge in Dublin on your morning show and I am very grateful to you for it. Yes, I am the mother of four children who was dazed on the floor, and my children looking at me. You were shocked when reading it, but, Gay, I could write a book of my life and it would be very ugly reading as it would contain very little happiness. I am not a bad housewife and mother but when you get repeated beatings, and most times you don't know what they were for, you begin to lose all confidence in yourself and you begin to believe it was your own fault, and you deserved it. You stay away from people and go into hiding until your black and blue marks have faded.

I can tell you that when my children were smaller, I used to find it very hard to lift them out of their cots as I was all pains after beatings. I could go on and on but I won't. All I will say to you is to thank you again for airing the phone numbers. If there are women out there listening and are being beaten, or abused in any way, use those numbers and get out fast as it won't stop but get worse.

For decades, Ireland and its citizens did not want to acknowledge something so upsetting as domestic abuse. It was preferable to sweep it under the rug and let women suffer alone in silence.

Dear Gay,

For years, I have endured a husband who outwardly seems charming, loves his drinking sessions, card sessions and GAA.

But, Gay, and this is the big but, once he gets inside his own door, the mood changes to one of aggression, bad language, violence. You name it and he has done it. Even though I don't get out to many social functions myself - over the years I have carried his and my share of the responsibilities - he loves to accuse me of all sorts of carrying-on - even opposite my children. I have often been locked out all night and at times have feared for my very life.

After years of struggling, trying to find understanding from doctors, priests and friends, all to no avail, I finally found an understanding male ear. He has been wonderful to me, caring, understanding and helpful in so many ways that only for him I would have lost my sanity long ago. I am staying with my husband for the sake of my children, whom I love dearly, and like the true loyal wife I am I cover for my professional husband's despicable behaviour.

He is so charming and helpful in his line of business to strangers that his sheer hypocrisy makes me fume inwardly.

Gay, please highlight this dreadful situation of wives as they get very little real understanding. We have the Catholic Marriage Advisory Committee who are a group of fuddy-duddies drawn from couples whose dull lives have never thrown up any real problems and who seem totally incapable of dealing with reality. Their involvement seems to be curiosity to find out how other people live, rather than in offering any real solutions. Please,

please, Gay, do not undermine the real suffering of these women - they are loyal, caring and wonderful women who would endure anything for the sake of their families but feel very much on their own, coping with such utterly selfish men - these so charming, wonderful beings to everybody outside their own domain.

Yours,

Some of the letters on this subject refer to 'street angels' and 'house devils': men who were model citizens publicly, but who became very different people at home.

Dear Gay,

I listen to your programme every morning and enjoy it enormously. Could you, would you, as a Christmas present to all us 'Cinderella wives' whose husbands are 'street angels and house devils', have a reputable psychiatrist on your programme to explain to us in the easiest way possible why these men behave as they do. My own explanation is that they are very insecure men. They are afraid to display their hostile emotions or disagreements whilst at work or on the street for fear of rejection, but these emotions must have an outlet and unfortunately all too often it is their wives and children who are the recipients. What these men need, besides the obvious, is to take up some form of sport where they can relieve themselves of their pent-up hostile emotions. Squash would be an ideal game as I'm sure the ball wouldn't object to being the receiver of so much anger and aggression. If these 'street angels' played a game of squash each evening before returning home to wife and children, and dumped the glass of whiskey down the sink, maybe our 'house devils' would turn into 'house angels'.

████████████.

Dear Gay,

I listen to your programme every morninge and enjoy it enormously.
Could you, would you as a Christmas present to all us "Cinderella
Wives" whose husbands are "street Angels" and house Devils" have a
reputable psychiatrist on your programme to explain to us in the
easiest way possible why these men behave as they do.
My own explanation is that bh they are very _insecure men_ . They
are afraid to display their haostile emotions or disagreements whilst
at work or on the street for fear of rejection but these emotions must
have an outlet and unfortunately all too often it is their wives and chi
who are the recipients.
What these men need, besides the obvious is to take up some form of
sport where they can relieve themselves of their pent-up hostile emotion
Squash would be an ideal game as I'm sure the ball would'nt object
to being the reciever of so much anger and agression.
If these "street Angels" played a game of squash each evening before
returning home to wife & Children, and dumped the glass of whiskey
down the sink, maybe our "house devils" would turn into "house angels"

████████████.

The theme of mental cruelty ran though many of these letters. The relentless undermining of this woman's self-esteem to breaking point is hard to read.

Dear Gay,

I was so interested in your programme on marriage last Wednesday. Everywhere there seems to be such unhappiness.

I was married to a man with whom I hardly had a happy day, who turned me from a cheerful, trusting girl to a mental wreck.

He then left me with no money and I had to make some kind of life for myself. It was difficult at first as I was untrained for any profession, but I did various jobs and finally a relation left me some money and I was able to set up a home.

I lacked the courage and initiative to leave years before. I was continually told how stupid I was and had absolutely no self-esteem. However, I managed and now everything is fine.

To give you a small example of the sort of man he was - on the way from the church to the reception, I asked him if he thought I looked nice. 'No,' he said, 'I don't.' I was taken aback. He said, 'I believe in being honest.' No more was then said. Our honeymoon was a disaster. We sat in expensive restaurants while I listened to stories of the beautiful models he used to take out: 'So different to you,' as he said.

You might well say 'Why on earth marry such a man?' I know, but during our engagement he seemed quite affectionate, and I thought that he loved me. He said so, until the evening before we married, when he said, 'You realise that you are fonder of me than I am of you.' He couldn't understand why I was hurt.

Strangely, I went on caring for this cold and sometimes violent man for several years. The odd thing is we now meet occasionally, and he is perfectly pleasant and we get on well. I remarked on this to him and he said, 'Well, you see, I am not married to you now and you no longer pose a threat.'

I don't know what one can learn from this, except that there are people who should never marry and to persevere in such marriages is a waste of time and life.

It's important to keep in mind that the subjects that Gay discussed on his show were not linear or independent of each other. Rather, each new story featured would unleash a new wave of letters and conversation related to and expanding the given subject. This letter, sent in the aftermath of the Ann Lovett tragedy in 1984, details one woman's suffering at the hands of an abusive husband. This writer was inspired to contact Gay on hearing the tragic news, identifying in some way with Ann and relating the story to her own marriage.

Dear Gay,

Your programme about rows in marriages enticed me to tell you of my experiences. I was very young and pregnant when I got married. Like Ann Lovett, I never knew the facts of life. I was just a mixed-up kid, and I had anorexia twice when I was a teenager. My husband comes from a very large family, all women. They and his mother idolise him. One of those mama's boys. Every time they visit, they talk to him all the time … and completely ignore me. He goes out every night for his drink and he often beats me up when he comes home. I said it to his mother one time that I was lonesome at night and that I'd like him to stay at home, but all she said was he deserved that, and I'm supposed to stay at home every night and mind his children. I had a nervous breakdown during the summer and all the time I was in hospital not one of the so-called 'outlaws' came to see me.

By the way, he always takes their side in any argument, and to tell you the truth, Gay, with every passing day I hate him more. I think there should be divorce in this country for people like me who had no choice in our lives. Please read out this letter soon, as I may not be around that much longer. What have I to live for?

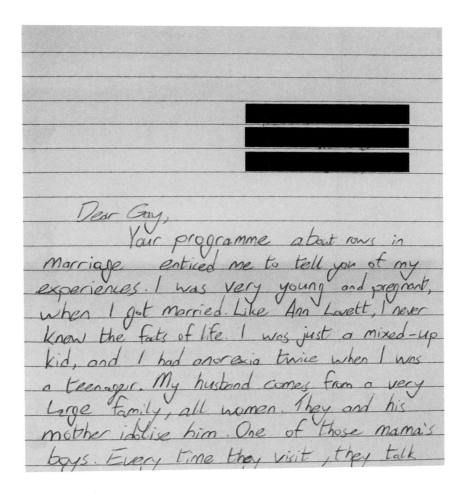

Dear Gay,
Your programme about rows in marriage enticed me to tell you of my experiences. I was very young and pregnant, when I got married. Like Ann Lovett, I never knew the facts of life. I was just a mixed-up kid, and I had anorexia twice when I was a teenager. My husband comes from a very large family, all women. They and his mother idolise him. One of those mama's boys. Every time they visit, they talk

<u>Please do not call out my full name or address</u>

███████████
██████████████

Dear Gay,

Bank Holiday The clock on my kitchen wall has just struck one a.m.
on ^Monday. In desperation I start to write this "cry from the heart"
to ^you! Its sudden chime frightened me, as everything seems to do
these times. My children are in bed asleep and dreaming sweet
dreams (I hope!)

No, I am <u>NOT a WIDOW</u>, in the accepted sense of the word.
At least a widow knows where her husband is and does <u>NOT</u>
dread his return! I am the wife of an alcoholic. At times, I
think that widowhood would be an escape from the hell in
which I and my children now live.

Before we were married my husband drank heavily, but
I assured myself that when we were married, with a home of
our own, that the pub would hold less attraction for him.

Alas! I was wrong. As the years went by and our
responsibilities increased, his drinking became progressively worse. I
have tried scolding him, threatening him, and praising him - all
to no avail.

I am weary covering up for him with his employer, with
my own family and with our neighbours. I try to keep the
best side out, when the final notice from the ESB arrives, and
when I have not enough money for my childrens schoolbooks.

However, I feel I cannot take anymore, now that my
husband has started to threaten me with physical violence,
sometimes in front of the children. They are already starting
to have problems at school, according to the school principal.

As I live in a small town, I feel that I have no one
to help me - no one would understand. None of my neighbours
have husbands like mine - I feel they would think that it was
all my fault, but I have tried everything.

Our GP is not interested - he is too busy to listen to
my litany of problems. Can any of your ^many listeners offer me
any glimmer of hope based on their own experience?

Yours in desperation
██████████████

Alcohol abuse was often a major factor in accounts of abusive husbands. Many letters in the RTÉ archives discuss alcoholism – a silent issue that so many families still struggle with today. Again, very little help was available to these women, who felt pressure from the wider community to keep up appearances and not complain publicly.

Gay would often acknowledge that the people listening were busy working in their homes. For letters such as this, he would introduce it by asking his listeners to stop what they were doing for a minute, and to sit down and listen. Their reactions in the following days would indicate that they did just that.

'This letter that I'm going to read to you now', says Gay on air, 'is, I'm afraid, probably representative of the way that many people live their lives. Listen to this.'

Dear Gay,

The clock on my kitchen wall has just struck 1 a.m. on a bank holiday Monday. In desperation I start to write this 'cry from the heart' to you. Its sudden chime frightened me, as everything seems to do these times. My children are in bed asleep and dreaming sweet dreams. (I hope!)

No, I am not a widow in the accepted sense of the word. At least a widow knows where her husband is and does not dread his return. I am the wife of an alcoholic. At times, I think that widowhood would be an escape from the hell in which I and my children now live.

Before we were married my husband drank heavily, but I assured myself that when we were married, with a home of our own, the pub would hold less attraction for him.

Alas! I was wrong. As the years went by and our responsibilities increased, his drinking became progressively worse. I have tried scolding him, threatening him, and praising him - all to no avail.

I am weary covering up for him with his employer, with my own family and with our neighbours. I try to keep the best side out, when the final notice from the ESB arrives, and when I have not enough money for my children's schoolbooks.

However, I feel I cannot take any more, now that my husband has started to threaten me with physical violence, sometimes in front of the children. They are already starting to have problems at school, according to the school principal.

As I live in a small town, I feel that I have no one to help me - no one would understand. None of my neighbours have husbands like mine - I feel they would think that it was all my fault, but I have tried everything.

Our GP is not interested - he is too busy to listen to my litany of problems. Can any of your many listeners offer me any glimmer of hope based on their own experience?

Yours in desperation,

When Gay read out a particular letter like this, the responses would pour in. How quickly people sat down to write their own letters is telling of the effect hearing a story so like their own had on them. When one woman was brave enough to speak out and share her story, very soon others took strength and communicated their own experiences. It is clear from the letters, and not just those about alcohol, that while so many women were suffering on their own, often in remote rural areas, it was hearing other women's experiences and realising that they weren't alone that gave so many of them the strength and the courage to try to change the course of their lives.

A rally organised by the anti-divorce lobby in Dublin in 1995. Those for and against turned out for the demonstration in Dublin in advance of the referendum vote.

30/10/86

Dear Gay

Thank you for reading out the ██████ letter ████████ about ████ alcoholic husband. Her letter could have been written by me and I'm sure thousands of other wives. Please don't drop the subject as its got to be the greatest scourge affecting our country. My husband

your show so ████ will learn from your ██ which he refuses to liste████ me.

████ with you that ████ are useless unl████ ██ carried out. ████ years dishing out ████ to my husband ████ I did not carr████ he simply doesn'████ any of them.

████ last few days I ████ told him that I will ████ him when I reach ██████ 30th birthday as ████

PS ████ Just ████ call me a listener.

Dear Gay,

Thank you for reading out the letter [...] about [the] alcoholic husband. The letter could have been written by me and I'm sure thousands of other wives. Please don't drop the subject as it's got to be the greatest scourge affecting our country. My husband listens to your show so maybe he will learn something from your programme which he simply refuses to listen to from me.

I agree with you that threats are useless unless they are carried out. I've spent years dishing out threats to my husband which I did not carry out. Now he simply doesn't believe any of them.

In the last few days I have told him that I will leave when I reach my 30th birthday, as by that time I will have wasted 10 years of my life on him. Maybe if he hears it over the air he will believe me. It will then be up to him to decide whether drink is worth losing his whole family for.

Yours sincerely,

Another letter, also concerning alcoholism, might have caught Gay's attention for a slightly different reason, and one he felt very passionately about – road safety.

Dear Gay,

I've a problem I'm sure a lot of your listeners will share with me - I'm married to a man who drinks.

Now that's alright because I like a drink myself. And my husband is not an alcoholic but the trouble is he gets very aggressive when he drinks and always insists on driving home when we've been out, even when he's well on. Unfortunately, I can't drive myself and things got very bad two Saturdays ago when we went to a 'do'. After a night's drinking he was almost footless and I decided to take the keys of the car off him. I told him we'd get a taxi home and he could collect it the following morning.

Well, Gay, a terrible row started. He got very abusive and I was humiliated in front of a crowd of people I know quite well. Because he was so drunk, I felt very sure of my ground and, anyway, I'd already ordered the taxi - the unfortunate taximan sat and waited while this public wrangle went on. It was so embarrassing. Anyway, to cut a long story short, we went home in the taxi in complete silence and my husband hasn't spoken to me since. I feel so small and belittled by his attitude, yet I know I did the right thing.

I love my husband - he can be great fun and he's a very good father to our three children but I saw an ugly side of him that night which genuinely surprised me and I'm very taken aback by the coldness of his attitude to me since - it's as if I publicly humiliated him by taking away the car keys, rather than the other way around. I know I'm going on a bit, but to make matters worse, my next-door neighbour and very good friend tells me I should apologise to him because I've undermined him. My school-going children all have bicycles and I constantly worry about them being on the road, so how can I honestly tell my husband he's right when I know in my heart he's a potential killer when he drinks like this and then he drives the car?

Forgive my long story, Gay, but I feel better already having told someone.

It goes without saying that alcohol abuse was not something that only men battled with. Another letter offers a different point of view: a woman's descent into alcoholism. But, like most of the best letters that Gay read out on air, it is an example of how it is nearly impossible to read these letters individually, without touching on a wider interconnected array of social and cultural circumstances of the time. In many ways, this long but deeply moving letter is the perfect microcosm of what life in Ireland was like for many women at this time.

Dear Gay,

I was a skinny, unattractive child from birth and one of those least 'favoured' in the family. My mother slaved for all of us, worked from dawn till dusk, and hardly ever spoke a kind word to any of us. She was always snapping at us and cried frequently. All this, of course, was because of my father, who was a non-event in my life anyway - do the day's work and escape to the pub in the evening. This was his lifestyle.

My mother had an obsession with academic qualifications, thinking mistakenly that by pushing the children they would have better lives than she had. Anyway, with pushing and shoving and roaring and threats, I was finally bamboozled through the Leaving Cert and passed with five honours. I walked out of school with no sense of self-esteem, love-starved, no confidence, giddy, immature - an ideal prey for any system which would help me escape from myself; a person I had come to hate.

An answer presented itself, of course. I was not long in the career my mother had chosen for me (my own choice would have been completely different) when I started to drink. This to me was the greatest discovery of all time. This was the real escape route … or so it seemed at the time. Living up the country and away from the watchful eyes of my mother, I met up with a 'wild gang' and, by the end of four years, I was well and truly on the road to early alcoholism.

Up to now, I had held on to my virginity and had also gotten dog's abuse from fellows from time to time because I wasn't 'game'. In spite of the drinking, Gay, I stayed clear of sex, not for virtuous or moral reasons, but because the notion that sex and my body were dirty and untouchable had been ingrained in the brain long ago, so the whole idea revolted me.

However, it eventually happened with a man who was older though just as inexperienced as I. Now, why did I have sex with this man? Not because I loved him. Oh no. I liked him alright and didn't want to lose him as he was the first human being who had ever showed me any real kindness. He began to get randy and, eventually, to stop him getting so irritable and sulky with me for not doing what he wanted, I gave in. At that stage, curiosity as well as a 'couldn't care less' attitude had set in. 'Was it nice?' you might ask. No, it was not. I screamed with pain and then just lay there while he relieved himself on me. Still, I had found a way to keep him from fighting with me and, after that, it was no big deal. I learned the natural methods of contraception and this did work for three years, mainly because he left me there for long periods of time anyway, but I didn't believe I deserved any better and accepted all of this as the norm.

Eventually, the inevitable happened. I found out that I was three months pregnant. Oddly enough, my man stood by me (if it could be called that). He wanted marriage straight away. I, on the other hand, had grave misgivings. We were both on the booze merry-go-round at this stage and I could only foresee disaster. I had absolutely no one whom I could turn to. I didn't trust anyone enough to tell them and to dare say I didn't want to marry this man. My mother or father were the last people on earth

I would have told and they didn't know I was pregnant before marriage until my little baby arrived and then both my parents and his family had a stroke. Baby was adopted, of course. Father never seemed to take much notice once the initial shock was over, but Mother has never really let me forget it.

[So many of our married] years were spent in the throes of my husband's active alcoholism (a form of hell which I would not wish on any other woman alive). I had stopped drinking once my first child was born. Life since my marriage has been one of demand-meeting. During the drinking years, through fear of my husband's violence and since out of habit, I don't know any better. I have no self-assertiveness. I ask nothing for myself. My husband lives his own life in his own little world and only comes to me to satisfy his demands. He still gets very irritable if things are not to his satisfaction.

However, I believe that out of every situation there comes some good. First of all, Gay, I had to start taking steps to control my fertility after my last child was born. I simply could take no more mentally or physically. I had been relying on the famous 'natural' methods and my husband's good will and co-operation. There was less and less of this as time went on and I really believed that he would have let me go through the torture and misery of pregnancy after pregnancy, but that I finally (and secretly) took the law into my own hands and asked my doctor for the pill. This was the best thing that ever happened to me. It's four years now since I had my last child. I have to stop the pill soon because of my age (36) but I'll then use the diaphragm. I intend to always have time for my children. I am bringing them up completely differently in every way to the way I was reared.

Some of the most private letters written by married women tell stories not of being trapped in abusive relationships or battling with an alcoholic partner, but simply of being stuck in loveless and sexless marriages. For various reasons, their husbands seem to show absolutely no interest in them. For many, this is the most isolating and lonely experience of all. These letters are remarkable in their illustration of Ireland slowly opening up after years of repression.

Sexless marriage

Letter 1

Friday 20th November

The Gay Byrne Show,
Radio Telefis Eireann,
Donnybrook,
Dublin 4.

Dear Gay,

   I listened with interest to your letter on Friday morning last regarding the lady who is sexually neglected. I thought it was me she was talking about.

   My Husband of five years has no interest whatsoever in sex, in fact I cry myself to sleep most nights from sexual frustration after making advances and being rejected yet again. He is cold, unloving and shows no affection towards me whatsoever. Im young, reasonable attractive and would have plenty of opportunity to get sexual relief elsewhere but Im just not interested as I love my Husband very much.

Do any of your listeners have any solutions to this type of problem?

Dear Gay,

I listened with interest to your letter on Friday morning last regarding the lady who is sexually neglected. I thought it was me she was talking about.

My husband of five years has no interest whatsoever in sex. In fact, I cry myself to sleep most nights from sexual frustration after making advances and being rejected yet again. He is cold, unloving and shows no affection towards me whatsoever. I'm young, reasonably attractive and would have plenty of opportunity to get sexual relief elsewhere but I'm just not interested as I love my husband very much. Do any of your listeners have any solutions to this type of problem?

Whatever about solutions to the problem, many of Gay's listeners were able to share similar situations where, for whatever reasons, they too had found themselves in a marriage where husband and wife did not have sex. Gay read out these letters on air, and as the conversation grew, more and more people were compelled to share their own unhappy stories. These responses reveal the misery of sexless marriages for both wives and husbands.

Dear Gay,

I have the same problem and I often wonder how my husband and I came by our children. Since the dreaded AIDS was mentioned we have not made love at all. That is over three years ago, if memory serves correctly. It was only once a year before that. This rejection was always painful for me and I am sure it worried my husband too.

Like your other listener I have never had sex outside marriage, although I've thought about it. I love my hubby very much and he loves me. I am in my forties now and my sex-drive is dying but I would still love a romp around the bed!

The mention of AIDS in the above response is interesting as it demonstrates, yet again, the various interconnected social issues that contributed to the culture of the time. The first cases of AIDS were diagnosed in Ireland in 1982. Such little information was known about the disease in these early days that it was easy for incorrect information to spread quickly through a community and the wider country, gripping many people in fear in the process.

Another issue that regularly appeared in the letters written to Gay was extramarital affairs.

We had a much better sex life before we got married, but in recent years my wife refuses to have sex with me at all. Worse still, although we can talk about everything else, she will not, cannot, talk about this. I love her very much and have tried everything I can think of to let her know how much I love her, and how special she is to me. To the rest of the world she is a sophisticated suburban housewife and nobody knows about this problem in our marriage.

She is very affectionate to our child, and hugs and kisses him. However, she can show me no physical affection whatsoever. I know that I am not dirty, ugly or unattractive, but my wife simply just cannot touch me. I would not dream of having an affair in Ireland, as I would be afraid to break up my family and hurt my wife, both of whom are very important to me. But when I travel abroad I do sleep with other women. It is all very adult. I do not say 'My wife does not understand me' because she understands me very well, and I think that she is relieved that I find solace sometimes with other women who actually enjoy sex. I continue to try to encourage my wife to show me physical love. I will not force her, and I won't fight with her about it. I grew up in a house where there were vicious arguments and I know how destructive

this can be for the children. However, my wife refuses to
go and see a marriage counsellor or a sex therapist about
this - like an alcoholic, she refuses to admit anything
is wrong. But I keep on hoping that, one day, she will be
able to love me as I think she wants to. Although physical
rejection is very hard to deal with, I believe that she
loves me, and I know that I love her very much.

Gay was receiving letters about affairs as early as 1983. One day he read out a letter by a woman who was contemplating having an affair with a married man. The letter compelled another woman, using the name 'Maria', to contact the show and share her story. She had recently discovered that her husband of 24 years was having an affair with another woman. It's a highly moving piece of radio. In many ways, it sounds like a private conversation between two people, except, of course, it takes place on national radio. Gay's exploration of the issue revealed complex, multi-layered and highly emotional experiences. Gay received letters from all points of view and from all over the country: people who, for various reasons, wanted to have affairs but wouldn't; people who were actively having affairs and people who found out that their partners were having affairs, and how they dealt with the fallout. Yet again, an unspoken truth – something that had been going on behind closed doors – was being broadcast for the first time.

A heartbreaking letter that came in response to Maria's interview is a good example of the community of listeners in conversation with each other. It's quite moving to see these people who do not know each other reach out and provide support.

Listening to your caller on Friday morning, I cried, Gay.
It was as if I was talking to you myself telling you my
story. I too had a loving, caring husband, who was also
my best friend. He was a marvellous father and I loved
him very much. We were married just 13 years and I was
seven months pregnant when one day he said to me that he
was having an affair with somebody I knew very well. It

wasn't at all like him. He never understood people who did this sort of thing to their partners, and he was totally against it always. Anyway, our baby was born, a lovely healthy boy, and I was home two weeks when he was looking for a separation. To this, I would not agree. I have two other children. I tried very hard to save our marriage. I clearly understood him falling in love with someone else as these things can happen. If we let them. I cried day and night for a year and a half. Many times I was going to drown myself, although there was always some occasion to stop me. I lost five stone and seven months from mental torture. I don't know where I got the strength to keep going. In the end, he walked out on me and on our three children. I forgave him twice and had him back only to do the same to us again. He is three months gone now as I write, and I wouldn't have him back again to put us through the same thing. Never again. He used to say the same things to me as Maria's husband said to her. My advice to her is to let him go. It's going to be hard, and very hard on her at first. But at least she will not go through the mental strain that I went through for 18 months, and all of it for nothing. If he does not want to be with her, she cannot hold him. And at the moment she thinks she could not live without him. I thought the same, tell her, but now I'm making a life of my own, and I'm very happy indeed, and so are my children. I will never forget our happy days, or the hurt I have gone through.

It wasn't just the wives who suffered; the women in relationships with married men also wrote to Gay about their experiences.

I've been having an affair [...] And because of the usual obligations, he too has returned to his wife. I'm 26 years old and I feel so despairing and miserable that it's as much as I can do to make it through each day. It seems such a waste of life that because of social stigma here in Ireland, both [he] and myself have to live in this utter misery. We still occasionally see one another and both of us usually end up in tears at the end of our meeting and the goodbye is inevitable. As well as the fact that [he] is married, he is also older than I am, which makes the situation even more precarious.

There is so much more emotion involved in an affair of this sort compared to a usual relationship, and it is no good for people to say that there are other fish in the sea. I loved and still love [him] so completely, and he has brought me the highest and lowest points in my life. There will never be a replacement. And I talk from experience, because he left me after the first six months, as he felt our relationship was holding me back and he felt guilty about family upsets. During the eight months of this absence, I never even looked at another man. Now that's happened again, I feel so numb, but I know that I will never give up. I love him. And if loving him means being in constant pain because of his marriage, then that's the way it has to be.

And regret was experienced not only by the women who lost the men they loved. This incredibly strong letter comes from a man who had an affair.

I have been listening to your programme re affairs. And as I have been there, done that and worn the T-shirt, I thought that my story might be of some interest to you and perhaps of some help to others. I got the 40-year itch, and there were a few brief encounters, which did not do anyone any harm because nobody found out about them. I should add, I was a reasonably successful businessman with the nice house, the Merc, the attractive wife, and lovely kids, happily married for 20 years. Anyway, myself and my wife went to a party one night and I became friendly with a lovely woman, happily married with five kids. We talked for the whole evening. And before she left with her husband, I asked her for her phone number. She looked at me with shock and disbelief and said 'no, no'. And left. Her number was in the book, and I rang the next day and said hi. She said, 'Who is this?' And I said, 'If you don't know, this is a wasted call.' She then said my name and within one month we were in a full-blown affair. I know now, 12 years down the road, that two mistakes were made at this stage: one, I made the call and, two, she did not hang up on me. You see, Gay, there are perpetrators and victims in all these situations. And I have no doubt at this stage that we were both perpetrators, and her husband and my wife were victims. I do believe that it was a first for both of us, and probably because of that we did not bail out in time. (That is, before we hurt other people.) Anyway, Gay, her husband loved his business. She claimed he was an alcoholic and, I don't know, perhaps he hit the bottle because of me. He lost his business, their home, everything, and moved away and left her in a rented house with children to rear. And the poor fella tried to be my friend while I was chasing his wife's tail. My wife, when she found out, tried to commit suicide and all hell broke loose. And I left a good woman, who loved me and my children, who suffered unbearable damage. And I would add here, Gay, that I have always supported my wife and children financially and my leaving did not affect them in any material way. Our affair lasted 10 years, Gay.

She got a job, reared her children very successfully, and although we never lived together because of her children, we went on holidays together and met regularly and planned [that] when her youngest child left the nest we would eventually have a house together. Well, Gay, our love came to a rocky period. I accused her of being unfaithful to me. Whether she was or not, I'll never know. But she's definitely capable of going for what she wants, and to hell with the consequences. From that time on, Gay, I went through six months of hell. Every phone call I was checking in on her, every bunch of flowers was an appeasement for something I had done or was about to do. Every loving touch a need for sex. I tried to get her to come away on holidays with me and I hoped to try to put together what we had. Every excuse under the sun was made and my begging was in vain. From being ten year[s] previously her lover, her friend, her confidant, I was now her victim. It was over, Gay. I told her, she cried. We parted. That's my story from where I am. The pain since leaving her is something unbearable. But I suffer that pain with dignity and self-respect, a privilege not afforded to me in the last months of our relationship. When I think of my pleading with her to come away to try to get our relationship back on the road, my mind goes back ten years to my own two little boys: one hanging out of my leg, the other with his arms around my waist. 'Home, home, Daddy, please come home. Mammy will do anything, Daddy, if only you will please come home.' And God forgive me because I never will. I walked away. I'm not looking for anyone's sympathy, and I don't need it. I have a good life. But if my letter could be of help to someone in the early stages of an affair, before any innocent parties are hurt, I would say to them what has been said by someone before me: learn from other people's mistakes, you won't get time to make them all yourself. If I had my chance again, I would suffer any pain before I would cause the pain I have inflicted in the name of love. Been there, done that.

Of the next letter on the programme, Gay knowingly said, 'And I would imagine that it might echo the lifestyle and the feelings of a good number of people around the country.'

I would like to tell you of my experience in the infidelity stakes. It may help you to understand another facet of the problem, which you are discussing at this present time; that is to say older, married man falling in love or otherwise having relations with young girls.

I am well into my 50s and I've been married almost 30 years. My work takes me away from home a lot, both inside and outside Ireland. Up to this present time, I've never even 'messed around', to use a modern phrase. I've always enjoyed admiring the opposite sex, but never in a lustful way. Indeed, that still stands. About five years ago, something happened. What, I don't know, but gradually it became painfully obvious to me that I seem no longer needed in my household, neither by my wife nor my children. I was there but I honestly didn't think that it would be noticed if I was not. Life went on. I recognised birthdays and other achievements. My wife and I went out together to our friends' homes and they came to us. Nothing was apparent on the surface. As a matter of fact, my friends often confided in me that they hoped they would always be as happy as we were. There were no fights, no arguments above and beyond the normal family tiffs. We stopped making love. Nothing dramatic, we just stopped. And on the surface life went on as normal. Many times, I thought of leaving - not relinquishing my responsibilities - just getting out and finding a flat somewhere on my own. I wasn't thinking of living with somebody else. There was no somebody else to think about. Neither did I think in terms of looking for somebody else. I just didn't want to be where I wasn't needed. I honestly thought that the only pain that would be caused was the pain of embarrassment my family would feel at explaining my departure.

Some months ago, in the odd ways of life, I met a young girl about the same age as my eldest daughter. We hailed from diametrically different backgrounds. We had nothing in common. She had relinquished her faith. I believe strongly in and get great comfort from my belief in God. She loved - I could almost say lived for - alcohol. I am teetotal. She loved dancing. I have two left feet. She loved the pop scene. I never got beyond Perry Como. She is uneducated. I don't say this in any derogatory sense, it's just a fact. I have a complete third-level education. She was unemployed. I have an excellent job. She was the product of a broken home. I never knew anything but a loving family background from my earliest years. She was hitching to Dublin and I gave her a lift, and we began to have chats and all of that sort of thing. We arranged to meet again and did so many times over the next few months. I honestly feel that I was a help to her. We had no secrets. She knew I was married, where I lived and who I worked for. Suddenly, my life seemed to have taken on a purpose again. It was probably the fact that I'd found someone who needed me, and she'd found someone she could talk to with no strings attached. I brought her away on some of my journeys with me, always booked her a separate room and just enjoyed her company. We did sleep together on a few occasions, but purely for the satisfaction of being close to someone who really needed me. Yes, we kissed and embraced and I don't deny I enjoyed it. But it was the pleasure of our company, the look of the light on her face when we met, the fact of being needed by her that gave me the greatest satisfaction of all. I managed to get her a job when she was out of a job. She never asked me for anything. Once when speaking to her, I discovered she had no money and would not have any until next dole day. I managed to slip £30 into her purse without her knowing. I got a letter from her three days later enclosing the money and asking me never to do that sort of thing again. Last week, I told my wife the whole story. I felt I had to do so and was amazed by her reaction. She said very little. But she wrote to me what could only be described as the most wonderful love letter I've ever received. This from somebody who for years had barely recognised my existence, telling me that she didn't realise I've been ostracised so much, and saying how much she needs me and how different the future would be. The sad part is that I am now numb. I did not experience the thrill that such a letter should give me, and I cannot bring myself to take on the role of an active spouse. I honestly don't know what I'm going to do. I feel sad that all that love was there, but no hint of it ever emerged. And now when it does, it seems to me to be too late. My reason for writing is that there are possibly many other married couples of around our age who have given up saying 'I love you' and are just taking each other for granted. My problem was, I think, that I need to feel needed, and no one ever bothered to tell me that I was. This may seem childish, but nevertheless, that's the way I am.

Finishing the letter, Gay says, 'And that's the letter now exactly as we got it, and there's something that you can think about for the rest of the day.'

It is important to remember that while these letters revealed many previously unspoken truths, some of Ireland's darkest secrets had still not yet come to light. It can be difficult to read these letters with the benefit of hindsight, but it is possible to sense murmurings of what was to come.

People were beginning to find their voices, starting to take a bold first step and tell their stories. But not even Gay was prepared for the tidal wave of emotions, deeply personal testimonies, outrage, grief and shock that was to come in 1984, when a young woman named Ann Lovett died during childbirth in a small town in County Longford. This story would drag into the light what many people already knew, and it would continue to gain momentum until the country was forced to reckon with some of its darkest secrets.

Mullingar deaths of schoolgirl mother and child

Girl, 15, dies after giving birth in field

by EMILY O'REILLY

A 15-YEAR-OLD Co Longford schoolgirl died last week after being

4

'Where is the Love?'

—

ON SATURDAY 4 FEBRUARY 1984, as that evening's *Late Late Show* drew to a close, Gay read aloud a headline from the front page of the *Sunday Tribune*, which was to publish the following day: 'Girl, 15, dies giving birth in a field'. To his shame, as he admitted on air the following Monday, he breezily skipped through other headlines and remarked, 'Nothing terribly exciting there.' This had been the first moment that much of the country heard of what, until that point, had been a local and private tragedy in a small town in Ireland's midlands, Granard, County Longford. Before long, though, the story, first broken by journalist Emily O'Reilly, would grip the nation and release an incredible public outpouring of grief, anger and disbelief.

On a cold, wet and windy January morning – 31 January 1984 – fifteen-year-old Ann Lovett left her family home, as she had always done, supposedly on her way to school. On this day, however, Ann did not go to school. Instead, she went to the village's local grotto, dedicated to the Virgin Mary. At about 4 p.m. that evening, the light already starting to fade, Ann Lovett was discovered by three boys on their way home from school. Lying on her back in her school uniform beside a statue of Saint Bernadette, she was barely conscious and she had haemorrhaged a lot of blood. At some point that afternoon she had given birth to a baby boy. The baby now lay dead near her, wrapped in her school coat. Her body had started to go into irreversible shock. Ann Lovett, aged 15, died just before 7 p.m. that evening.

Ann's death came at a particularly contentious and divided moment in the country's history. Just four months earlier, in September 1983, Ireland had held a referendum in which a two-thirds majority had voted to formally recognise the equal right to life of the pregnant woman and the unborn child. The Eighth Amendment of the constitution was signed into law in October 1983. The result, which effectively embedded a ban on abortion into the constitution, came after a bitter referendum campaign. Eileen Carter, who wrote to *The Gay Byrne Show* following the death of Ann Lovett, described the 'hysterical' public reactions in the lead-up to the vote. While the amendment had been positioned as a way of protecting both mothers and their babies, Ireland in the 1980s was in reality an unkind, unwelcoming place for so-called 'unmarried mothers'. 'There have been Ann Lovetts in the past and there will be more in the future,' she wrote. Eileen was right. All over the country, unmarried mothers and other women connected to them – their mothers, sisters and friends – had suffered in silence long enough. They weren't going to be silenced any longer.

At the time, Kevin O'Connor was a reporter for *The Gay Byrne Show*. The day after the Ann Lovett story broke, O'Connor broadcast his report to the show from Granard. My own mother still says that she will never forget hearing it – anyone listening would have been stopped in their tracks. Writer Colm Tóibín described the report as 'factual and fair', and said that '[O'Connor] tried to give a sense of the town, of the context'. When you listen back to it today, O'Connor's report is almost detached – it was not a time for exaggeration. What he describes is almost poetic in itself – the religious references, the dominant position of the grotto outside the town. 'The grotto', he says, 'is to Our Lady of Lourdes. ... It's up outside the town. It looks down on the town. When [Ann] was up there, she would have looked down on her own life and the town, the people she knew.' He describes local people's reaction to the tragedy: 'Some people are offended by the term "field". Technically, it is a field. It is not part of the grotto. It's a little wooded area beside the grotto. But it was put very strongly by a friend of Ann's that she died on consecrated ground, and that she didn't die in a field. And that's important to people: the knowledge that she died on consecrated ground.'

O'Connor's report from Granard – the personal tragedy, the presence of religious iconography, combined with the difficult background of the recent referendum – sparked major reaction from listeners. It served as a springboard for the hundreds of letters that would descend on RTÉ studios in the following days. 'We've had an astonishing number of letters from all over the country, and indeed from outside the country, from people expressing their opinions about the situation, about the tragedy, and about their own attitude to it, and we think they make fascinating reading,' Gay told listeners. 'Too many letters came in to us for us to ignore them.'

On 23 February, Gay devoted the entire programme to simply reading out the letters, mostly from women, who were moved by the tragedy of Ann Lovett. The show was meticulously planned and executed, with the full backing of Gay's producer, John Caden. From the sackfuls of letters that had been received, Kevin O'Connor selected those to be read. Gay, along with two actresses – one with a middle-class Dublin accent; the other with a more rural one – simply read out the letters one after the other. Gay made absolutely no comment on them – he knew that they could and should speak for themselves. Most of the letters were first-person accounts from people who had gone through similar experiences, or stories of family members and friends. The subject jarred completely with the accepted version of reality that Ireland was trying to project at the time. All was not as it seemed – a dark side was erupting and could not be ignored.

Of the programme, Gay said: 'I believe that if *The Gay Byrne Show* has had influence, this is how it has been done – by doing programmes like this, allowing reality to show through the veils of hypocrisy, because by hearing everyday layers of opinions different from their own, people realise there are different legitimate points of view, other tolerances, other ways of approach.'

Reading out the letters on air exposed the previously untold anguish of women right across the country – women who, in many cases, had never told their story to anyone. Writing about the Ann Lovett programme for *Magill* magazine in 1984, Colm Tóibín said, 'There was an intense calm about the way he spoke, a controlled anger almost. ... Gay Byrne summed it up. He left us in no doubt. It has been his finest hour.' The letters received – so many with personal accounts of

Ann Lovett died aged 15 on 31 January 1984.

sexual abuse, infanticide, ignorance and fear – revealed a shocked, angry country grappling with how such a tragedy could have unfolded in this unassuming rural town. It sparked a nationwide debate that would continue to the present day.

Two blue boxes, marked simply 'Ann Lovett Letters', were handed to me by RTÉ archivists. These were Pandora's boxes, and the privilege of reading their contents was without a doubt the most incredibly powerful experience during my collation of *Dear Gay*. The letters convey the complete lack of information and education around sex in Ireland at the time. It simply wasn't discussed. And while many may have believed that this was to protect young women, in reality it had the opposite effect. This writer admits that she understood nothing of sexual intercourse, menstruation and childbirth, and it left her consumed by fear and guilt.

> The death of this young mother and her baby is the saddest story I've ever heard. No one except the people who have been there can ever hope to understand the hell hole she lived in all that time. She lived in a pit of black ignorance and she was simply, but heartbreakingly, a victim of ignorance. It brought me back to terror and paralysing fear that goes beyond pain and panic when I was 14. You can only understand the nature of ignorance when you too have been a victim.
>
> I'm finding it hard to tell you this, but I understand poor Ann very well, for I thought I was pregnant when I was about 14. I lived through hell because I couldn't get the information I desperately needed anywhere. I'm now in my twenties and I cannot believe that the information I so desperately needed is still not available to girls of that age or, indeed, any age today. In my case, a man had molested me for a few years, starting when I was 11. He continued to bother me and, although I was terrified, often I was even more terrified of telling my parents about him. When I learned that the thing that happened between men and women, as it was locally known, was

happening to me, I slowly began to understand that maybe I was also going to have a baby.

Two pieces of information were missing here: one is that there was not full penetration and, two, I had not yet started my periods. I didn't even know that it was biologically not possible for me to be pregnant. In total terror and panic I tried to find out from the newspapers any snippets of information. I read that babies like the one I would have were usually placed in brown paper bags and left in a toilet. I resolved to do this. It never occurred to me at any time that this baby would be a living human being. For that reason, I started to carry around the one penny I would need to get into the toilet to have the baby. I also kept a towel by my feet in my bed to mop up the blood, if I should be unlucky and it should be born in the night. I kept the brown paper bag in my school bag and kept the bag under my bed at night. No one ever even guessed that I was living in hell. My marks at school went up and down. And since I spent most of my time in the chapel praying, the nuns told me I had a vocation. I had no understanding of life. I didn't even know that a body could swell up with a baby, as the Virgin Mary never had any physical manifestations of her pregnancy. Also, my mother, who was very fat, had ten children, nine after me, and she never looked any different. I never saw babies as being special. My mother and father just seemed to ignore them most of the time. I really had no idea that babies were real people. I just viewed this baby I would have as something to be disposed of without telling anybody and without anyone finding out.

I made a point of watching the baby calves being born and it never occurred to me that there would be pain.

I was transfixed by the presence of blood at the birth because the sight of blood might raise suspicions. I can't begin to tell you what this long-drawn-out nightmare was like for me. It sucked all the life out of me for about two years. I didn't even know that the waiting period was nine months. And yet I continued to be the class clown, the court jester in the lives of my family and friends. I now look back with deep anger at my Catholic upbringing. It was so full of ignorance, secrecy, superstition, fear, terror, blind and wilful obedience. Outwardly, I played the part of the perfect schoolgirl, daughter, friend, Child of Mary. Yet inwardly I was dying of pain and panic and terror and shock, and no one ever knew. Sometimes, even now, I find this hard to believe, but not one person even suspected that I was trying to die. And I was praying to God that he would call me and I would get killed by a bus or in some accident.

I'm now very angry at the Catholic Church because we are all sad victims of her harsh, unfeeling and insensitive policies. If I'd really been pregnant at 14, I undoubtedly would have been another Ann. I don't blame my parents. They, too, had been victims of the same ignorance. Sex was absolutely out in those days. You just didn't dare breathe it. Everything connected with sex was a sin. Even knowledge connected with knowing about sex was seen to be a sin. I was a victim of one little word: ignorance. A few bits of information would have spared me an unimaginable nightmare. My mind was demented. And I still bear the scars of that time.

I should always be a nervous person, with awful and sudden fears, although everybody sees me as a happy and cheerful and kind nurse. Hearing of our little friend and mother Ann has reminded me of what it's like to be trapped in the hellhole of Catholic ignorance. We used to call it innocence.

One thing I do know is that I will never let nuns or priests near my children. They will not be taught the wrong ideas about life from a cruel church. I do hope you will read my letter but not my name. I would die for I still feel shame about the baby episode in my life. Yet. It was all caused by ignorance.

So many women lived in fear, simply because they were never told the 'facts of life', as many of the letters describe it.

Dear Gay,

I was watching *Today Tonight* last night on RTÉ 1. It gave a great many details about that poor little schoolgirl, Anne Lovett.

This holy Ireland rubbish has made many a poor girl leave home and go to England for abortion. Why had this poor little girl to die in the first place? [...]

Going back to my own youth, as I had no mother but had three older sisters, one married, I was never told anything about anything.

When I had my first period, in the month of August, I was fourteen years old.

To say that I was terrified, and horrified, was to put it very mildly indeed. I had no one to tell. So I was in a bad state when six days passed.

I knew absolutely nothing about it. I thought I had cancer. Luckily, it was school holidays. When it stopped, I was so relieved. Being brought up, as I had been, not to mention anything about babies or anything else, I could not possibly know that it was a natural event. I suffered martyrdom.

When it stopped, I, in my innocence, thought that was the end of my trouble. But, after another month, it started again. I was again terrified, and really thought I had cancer. I could confide in no one. So I suffered on, in dread.

After I had them for a year, some girls in school asked me if I had bleeding every month. I shyly answered 'yes'. I bless the girl who told me, 'We all have it.' That put an end to my awful worry. When my own only daughter came to me with her first period, I was able to reassure her, thanks be to God. But, if my own mother had been alive, I know she would not have told me, either.

Even after my marriage, when I became pregnant, I still knew nothing. I did not know how babies were born.

When I was taken into the hospital at about 8 p.m., I was so embarrassed. The young nurses laughed at me. I had a terribly hard labour for about three days. I got up, eventually, hardly able to walk. I shall never forget, or even forgive, those silly people who were responsible for all my suffering.

So, I am particularly sorry for that young child, and she was only a child, who has died in Granard. It could have been prevented. But maybe she had a mother like mine, and sisters like mine. I will pray for her every night. The father, as usual, gets off scot free … To this day I still shudder, when I think of my experience.

The Ann Lovett tragedy brought a huge wave of media coverage to Granard. Many locals did not appreciate this new-found attention, and they were reluctant to speak to reporters at all. Many people felt that the national media blamed them specifically for what had happened to Ann, and they were indignant that their small town – and what they believed should have been a private tragedy – was now splashed across front pages all over the country.

The grotto in Granard.

Dear Gay,

I have just listened to your program. Tuesday 7 February. I cried for that poor girl Ann and the torment she must have gone through. I also felt anger at the girl's family and neighbours of her town. Ten years ago I found I was pregnant. When I told my mother the first thing she said was 'what will the neighbours think, especially Mrs X, Y and Z? You have disgraced this house', and I was shown the door.

The father of my baby said he would stand by me. I left my home then and, four months later, we were married in a (UK) Registry Office. When my son was born I wrote to my mother and told her but she did not reply. Two years passed until I got a letter from my home. She (my mother) reminded me of the shame I had brought onto the house and in the same tone told me my father had had an

On 12 February, Canon Gilfillan, Granard's parish priest, delivered a sermon during that Sunday's Mass. In it, he criticised the national media's attention on the local town: 'What happened should have been left to the town to deal with in its own way. My firm belief is what happened should not have been covered by RTÉ or the newspapers: it should have been kept parochial, local,' he said.

Looking back on the coverage, Gay himself explained that 'among the very strong letters we received after the death of Ann Lovett would have been a whole host of letters saying: "You're making all this up ... This never happened. This is total nonsense. It's the D4 media again concocting stories." Those letters are a perfect depiction of the sort of Ireland we lived in at that time.'

Gay was right. These types of letters and, similarly, the parish priest's sermon are demonstrative of the culture of silence that existed in Ireland at the time. People all over the country, not just in Granard, did not want to know about what was really happening. That culture of silence brought with it a culture of shame, which in turn led to a fear of the social stigma that would attach to a family when a young woman 'got into trouble' by getting pregnant. Many lived in fear: fear of bringing shame on themselves or on their families; fear of upsetting the status quo; and, as a result, fear of being vilified and rejected by their own society.

Dear Gay Byrne,
I have just listened to your programme, Tuesday 7 February. I cried for that poor girl Ann and the torment she must have gone through. I also felt anger at the girl's family and neighbours of her town. Ten years ago, I found I was pregnant. When I told my mother the first thing she said was 'what will the neighbours think, especially Mrs X, Y and Z? You have disgraced this house', and I was shown the door.

The father of my baby said he would stand by me. I left my home then and, four months later, we were married in a [UK] Registry Office. When my son was born I wrote to my mother and told her but she did not reply. Two years passed until I got a letter from my home. She (my mother) reminded me of the shame I had brought onto the house and in the same tone told me my father had had an accident and would I come home, as the neighbours were saying: 'How strange I hadn't come home to see my father, when he's so ill.' I don't know what story they told when I left home earlier.

All I say is no wonder that poor girl didn't tell anyone. I feel my parents didn't love me at all. Their sole concern was for the neighbours, not what would happen to me. At 19 years old, I left home, pregnant, hardly any money, but with a man who stood by me. He never stopped telling me he loved me and that everything would work out. Now, ten years later, I have a little girl and we have our own house. My husband has worked very hard those last ten years. We have never asked for a penny off my parents, nor was any help offered. My children have seen their grandparents four times in the last ten years but they were always embarrassed and couldn't wait for us to go.

My children and husband are treated as if we committed a terrible thing, but I think the terrible thing was committed by my parents.

It was clear from the letters that were coming in that Ann Lovett's situation was not unique, and neither was it a new phenomenon. Some letters proved that women had been having children outside marriage – and suffering the consequences – for generations.

Dear Sir,
It is with a heavy heart that I write. Part of me was sad for what Ann and her baby experienced. Part of me was happy for her and her little one.

My mum was an illegitimate baby just like Ann was trying to conceal. I watched her suffer to great extremes: being omitted from family occasions and all the snide remarks, not to mention the fact that my mum's mother left her behind to go to England, where she married happily and was well off. I was to witness her on holiday - her polite but evasive attitude to my mam.

Is it any wonder that my mam was to die at a very young age in a mental hospital?

Forgive them, Lord, for surely they must not know what they do.

The period leading up to the Eighth Amendment to the Irish constitution, signed into law just a few months before Ann Lovett died, had been a divisive and difficult time for many people in Ireland. In this letter, a young woman decides that it would be best if she travelled to England to seek an abortion. The culture of shame that existed in Ireland, which made women like her feel as though they had no choice but to travel for an abortion, is incredibly sad.

Dear Gay,
I feel I must tell you my story.

Last year I found myself pregnant. Before the result was confirmed I informed my boyfriend that I might be pregnant. We both agreed that if I was, we would get married and I would have our baby. The result was positive. I confided in my two sisters, who advised me not to continue with the pregnancy - it would break my mother's heart and would kill my father. What would the neighbours think? You would be made to feel so ashamed.

So after a lot of tears and talks, I finally decided that it was the best thing under the circumstances. My boyfriend and I flew to England five days later. I have two sisters living over in England and although they didn't approve of what I was about to do, they didn't stand in my way. I had the abortion in a private nursing home in London.

My point is that although I took the easy way out at the time - well, technically, it was the easy way out - but I took it upon myself to terminate the right to life of my unborn baby, and then I call myself a Christian. If I had been strong enough at that time, I would probably have told my parents, and although I believe it would have hurt them enormously, I also believe they would have come to terms and accepted the situation as it was. I would have kept the baby, and to hell with the neighbours. What's wrong with this country is that these kinds of things are happening every day, but we brush it under the carpet, and pretend it doesn't exist, when in actual fact we should talk openly about it, and accept it. It's nothing to be ashamed of. There are worse things happening in this country than having a baby outside of marriage, and feeling that you have to apologise to society for your mistake.

All I can say is that any girl who may find herself in such a situation should think before she acts. You are entitled to keep your baby - your own flesh and blood - just as much as any woman with a marriage certificate. That is your right, and the right of your child.

You must be sick and tired of getting letters in about the same subject, but I would appreciate if you read it out over the air. I am 21 years of age and feel very strongly about the subject.

All I cay say is that any Girl who may find herself in such
a situation, should think before she acts. "You are entitled
to keep your Baby - your own Flesh and Blood just as much as
any Woman with a Marriage Certificate. That is your Right, and
the right of your Child.

You must be sick and tired of getting Letters in,about
the same subject, but I would appreciate if you read it out
over the Air. I an 2I years of age, and feel very strongly
about the Subject.

Thanking You ,

Yours faithfully,
████████████

ANNE LOVETT FILE

The Eighth Amendment was signed into law in 1983.

The following story of 'Mary', a 'servant girl', is particularly shocking and distressing. In all these instances, only the women are blamed for their pregnancies. Very little is mentioned of the men involved and, in many cases, they get away without any responsibility or consequence.

As I drop you this line, my heart is so sad for poor little Ann Lovett. I know Our Lady took them both to Heaven in her arms.

A particular case that will always remain in my mind - in about 1940, Mary was an agricultural working girl, known then as a servant girl, employed by a farmer in this area. Mary (like all her equals) worked about 12 or 13 hours a day, beginning at six o'clock in the morning by lighting the fire, then off out to milk about ten cows, then in to get the breakfast for about three other working men and the employer and his family. Mary then helped to get the six children out to school, then clean up after all that, next out again and help to feed about fifty calves out of buckets, then wash the milk churns. In again to the house, start to prepare the dinner and other household chores and again clean up and start off again milking and feeding calves and finally the tea and the clean-up. There was no tap water. There were no hoovers or washing machines.

Mary became pregnant, like so many of these poor agricultural slaves. Mary's lover was a married man from a nearby village - the father of nine children. Mary was 28 years of age, a beautiful singer and always in good humour. Mary was able to hide her pregnancy until about the seventh month when one day the farmer's wife (who was also pregnant) confronted Mary. Mary denied everything and said her body gathered fluid sometimes and it disappeared again. Mary's employer didn't really believe this, but since Mary couldn't be replaced easily, a blind eye was turned to the situation. Mary continued with her work.

A day or two before Good Friday in that year, it was potato-setting day. All these potatoes were sown by hand, which meant everyone gave a hand, including Mary. Mary rushed into the house just before dinner to give the final help to serving up the meal for all the others. She had none herself, as she said she had a headache. She then cleaned and washed up after the meal and asked for an hour or two off to go to bed with this blinding headache. Mary got the permission and after about an hour, her employer called to her bedroom door which was locked. Mary assured her that she was much better and would be up shortly. After about another hour, the house was filled with the screams of a new baby. The employer went to the garden for her husband. He set off to Mary's house a few miles away and brought back her elderly father. Mary still had the door locked, and after they forced it open she denied everything. They searched the room and found a little baby boy, choked by a stocking and packed with her clothes in her case.

This father walked his daughter home and carried the case and later that night the baby was buried in the nearby graveyard. Mary had returned to her work after two days. I can assure you, she got no sympathy or concession. She kept her aches to herself. After two or three weeks, Mary had to visit a doctor. She was sent to the County Home Hospital for treatment. She again returned to her job on her discharge from hospital. She worked from dawn to dusk. Her distress, her broken heart, were all hidden in her heart. She got no help or care. It didn't exist then.

This is Mary's story. Mary is my aunt.

From as early as the 1920s, mother and baby homes had been set up around Ireland. They were run by various religious orders, mostly Catholic nuns, and funded by the Irish government. These institutions were set up to house 'fallen women' – women who became pregnant outside marriage. Even after the programme dedicated to reading out letters about Ann Lovett had aired, Gay continued to receive letters from listeners on the subject. It seemed that every letter read out would release a fresh wave of stories. Gay's listeners were listening to each other, and as each story was shared, someone else found the courage to tell theirs. Slowly, letters began to hint at the fact that all was not as it seemed in these homes.

Dear Gay,
Just listening to your programme of a selection of letters about Ann Lovett (RIP).
    Before I married, I was a nurse. In the early '70s I was between jobs and was told there were vacancies at

the unmarried mothers' home on the Navan Road, Dublin. Well, Gay, my dad drove me up to see the matron of the same place.

While waiting to see the matron, I was left standing in a corridor outside a kitchen door. There were pregnant girls pushing big baskets of laundry and scrubbing floors. A nun came up the corridor, gave me a look like a summons, went into the kitchen and said to whoever was there: 'another slut outside the door'. Well, Gay, all I was thankful for was that I wasn't there to have a baby. I was so cross, I told them what to do with their job.

Of course, it would be some time before the true horrors of what was happening behind the closed doors of these 'mother and baby' homes would be revealed.

The tragedy of Ann Lovett caught the country's imagination in a way that many could never have thought possible. To this day, the circumstances of Ann's death are a source of great pain and distress to many. But after many years of suffering in silence, people were ready to talk. Slowly, they were finding the courage to come together – emboldened by what they heard of each other on the airwaves – to speak out and share their stories.

Reflecting on the period years later, Gay said: 'Up to then we lived in Holy Catholic Ireland. Nothing ever went wrong. Everybody loved everybody else, and we knew where we stood in society. Everything was grand. Suddenly we got a quick peek under the stones and slabs as to what was going on all over the place.' Ireland's veil was gradually being pulled back. Gay, and the country at large, was ready to listen. Years later, of the letters that Gay received about Ann Lovett, and what they resulted in, Gay said: 'Time and again they make the point that being able to write it all down is a relief. They thank Ann Lovett for giving them the courage to express what they have kept secret. Her sacrifice was not in vain, is their point.'

5

Somebody's Child

—

BY THE 1980S, Gay's relationship with the people of Ireland was such that they began to write more deeply personal and confessional letters, often anonymously, revealing stories and personal experiences that gave us the first glimpses of a darker, more sinister side to holy Catholic Ireland: the treatment of unmarried mothers, sexless marriages, extramarital affairs, and domestic and sexual abuse. Gay would never dare claim that he was leading the way on any of this social change – he saw himself simply as enabling his many listeners to converse with and support each other. But Gay's listeners were far from finished yet.

The far-reaching influence of the Catholic Church in Irish society resulted in communities around the country controlled by shame – the fear of bringing shame on one's family or embarrassing the family in front of neighbours was a common concern addressed in so many of the letters that Gay received. Young girls and women who became pregnant outside marriage would often be sent away to mother and baby homes, set up in the early 1900s by religious orders, to have their babies away from the prying eyes of the community. Most of these innocent girls were accused of 'promiscuity', but it should be acknowledged that, in a significant proportion of cases, they became pregnant as a result of sex abuse or rape. Others very much loved the men with whom they had meaningful relationships, but because they were not married, they had brought shame on the family and so were sent away. Of course, many found that when they became pregnant, the men simply walked away. Irish society did not hold men accountable for pregnancy. Sex outside marriage was the very worst sin. Now these women and girls – victims, sisters, mothers, daughters – were forced to pay a terrible price.

Almost all the women in these homes were first-time mothers, usually in their teens, who, as seen in the letters, knew little of the 'facts of life'. Removed from their homes, families and all that was familiar to them, they were completely unprepared for the process of giving birth. And, in the majority of cases, without the support (financial or otherwise) of their families, it was almost impossible for unmarried mothers and their babies to stay together. Following the legislation on adoption in 1953, the most likely outcome for most of their babies was that they would be given up for adoption; others were fostered or raised in mother and baby homes.

The full extent of the desolate conditions of these homes, and the abuse that took place inside them, would not become public knowledge for many more years. Today, successive Irish governments are still grappling with how to remedy the atrocities of this dark chapter of Irish history. It's important to read the letters that were sent to Gay with an awareness of the social and cultural context of the time in which they were sent. While the abuse in these homes was not openly spoken about, the letters were our first glimpse as a nation into what was going on inside these buildings, and the impossible situation in which so many young women found themselves.

In 1986, Gay and his team featured a story about Tom Redmond, a man based in Stoke-on-Trent who had been adopted as a child. On air, Tom shared his story of trying to locate his birth family. As with many subjects discussed on *The Gay Byrne Show*, Tom's story caught many listeners' attention. 'We know very well from your letters after Tom was with us,' Gay says on air, 'that a lot of you, our listeners, felt particularly close to what Tom said, for all sorts of reasons.'

One person who heard Tom's story and who felt compelled to share their own story with Gay was Hugh Leonard, the well-known dramatist, television writer and columnist.

Dear Gay,

I take typewriter in fist to thank you for the lovely warm interview with Tom of Stoke-on-Trent. It has quite made my day - and it's only 11.05 a.m.

I was especially interested, for reasons of which you are probably aware. A few years ago, curiosity impelled me to engage an enquiry agent in an attempt to find out whence I came. It wasn't an obsession; I don't have any <u>conscious</u> hang-ups (more on that underlining in a moment), but it always nagged me. Once, when young, I actually half-believed that Denis Johnson was my true father! Anyway, the only things this Sam Spade had to go on was my mother's name, Annie (not given as Anne or Ann, but Annie, which suggests humble circumstances), a date of birth […] and an address on the North Circular Road.

This proved to be what was called a 'common lodging house': a kind of temporary resting place for mothers waiting their time. No register was kept, and if there had been one there is no doubt that the addresses given would be for the most part fictitious. So, the trail came to a dead end.

Forgive the preamble. Why I'm writing is that I think it might be a worthwhile thing if you were to investigate the terrible trauma which being adopted leads to. I underlined 'conscious' above, because the child who has been rejected by his or her mother - for whatever worthy reason - must find his entire outlook on the world forever coloured, even if he or she isn't aware of it. We all of us get kicked in the arse: a girlfriend, a wife, a business partner - in your own case, the betrayal by a close friend produced shock waves from which you feel you will never recover. Think, then, of the enormity of a rejection which comes when you are hardly out of the womb. I know girls who have been persuaded to give their babies away, as 'the best thing for you and it'. I don't believe this for a moment.

From the vantage point of age, I can look back on my own behaviour and attitudes (personal stuff), and without using these as an alibi, put the blame squarely on being, as they would say in the lane where I grew up, a 'nurse child'. And, of course, there is a positive side to the matter: if you are not the kind who goes under, then being adopted lights a fire under you: you want to prove yourself. Like that car rental firm, you try harder.

I lose sight of my point. Again, what I am suggesting is that underneath a normal, cheery, well-adjusted facade, such as that of Tom Redmond, there must be an abiding, if unacknowledged pain. I think the emphasis is on: what should the mother do? Rather than on: how will the adult cope with having been given away when young? In short, the child has become a 'thing'.

I hope you think it worth 20 minutes of airtime. As always, the show is a delight and keeps me from my labours.

Yours,

Hugh was well-known for his strong opinions, which regularly generated reaction and discussion. The next letter was no different. Gay knew that when he read it out, it would provoke a huge response – and it did. The letters in the files from the weeks after Leonard's letter came from the heart; their words so full of emotion.

Dear Gay,
I am 15 years old and I am adopted. While listening to the Gay Byrne hour on Monday morning I heard an excerpt from a programme in which Hugh Leonard was speaking about adoption. To put it quite frankly, Gay, this man makes me sick.

He mentioned that when he was a young boy, people used to say to him that he was rejected by his real mother when he was a baby. He then went on to say that adopted children feel rejected. Well, I can tell you this, Gay, even though I am adopted I do not feel in the least bit rejected. I am part of a happy family and my parents are very good to me. I have no sisters but my brothers do not make me feel like the odd one out or anything. I feel I am part of this family, as if I always have been.

I think that Hugh Leonard has no right to say things like this just because of his own experiences. When I grow older, I have permission from my adoptive parents to find my real parents if I want to. Maybe I will, but this does not worry me at present. If my parents do not want to meet me, I will understand. I am sure that they had a perfectly good reason for giving me up for adoption in the first place. But until then, I am quite happy to stay as I am.

I am in 4th year at school and I will be doing my intercertificate this June. My classmates know that I am adopted but they do not treat me any differently because of this. I enjoy playing the piano and my parents pay for me to have lessons. I have now completed my 7th-grade exam. In these exams I have got honours in all except one, in which I got a high merit.

Last August, my mother took me to America for a three-week holiday and we enjoyed ourselves thoroughly. I also went on holiday to Scotland a couple of years ago. So, as you can see, Gay, I lead a perfectly normal life and I do not feel rejected in any way.

I hope that my adoptive parents will always be proud of me.

Yours sincerely,

re ADOPTION

Dear Gay,

███████████████. I am 15 years old and I am adopted. While listening to the Gay Byrne hour on Monday morning I heard an excerpt from a programme in which Hugh Leonard was speaking about adoption. To put it quite frankly Gay, this man makes me sick.

He mention that when he was a young boy, people used to say to him that he was rejected by his real mother when he was a baby. He then went on to say that adopted children feel rejected. Well, I can tell you this Gay, even thoug I am adopted I do not feel in the least bit rejected. I am part of a happy family and my parent are very good to me. I have no sisters but my brothers do not make me feel like the odd one out

-3

ast August my mother took me
verica for 3 weeks holidays
we enjoyed ourselves
ghly. I also went on holidays
ttland a couple of years ago.
you can see Gay, I lead
le and I do not feel
I hope that my adoptive
mroud of me.

I am part of
always have been.
Hugh Leonard
things like
hui own
ou older I
eents to find
ill, but this
ents do not
swee that

ppy to stay as I am. ...ace. But until then I
I am in 4th year at school
and I will be doing my intercertificate this
June. My classmates know that I am adopted but
they do not treat me any differently because of this.
I enjoy playing the piano and my parents pay for
me to have lessons. I have now completed my 7th
grade exam. In these exams I have got honours
in all except one, in which I got a high merit.

When deciding what to air on the radio show each day, Gay always wanted to be led by his listeners. Whatever they wanted to talk about, whatever was important to them at any given time, is what would dictate the show's running order. Adoption was no different – it's clear from the number of letters in the RTÉ archives that this was something that many people felt strongly about and wanted to speak on.

Reading letters like this in 2023, from a child just like me in 1986, was an emotional experience. My sister, Crona, and I are both adopted. This is something that's always been known to us. I never remember being told about it specifically, nor do I remember any big deal ever being made of it. Adoption was common to many at the time, and because it was well known and normalised in our home, perhaps it helped others to think nothing of it in theirs, too. Ours was a truly happy home – chats about adoption never felt relevant to me. If anything, I only ever felt loved and, on reflection, incredibly lucky, too.

If *The Gay Byrne Show* were on air today, I believe that I would probably write of one particular memory I have: a simple question, which meant nothing to the child who asked it, but the answer meant the world to me.

One Saturday morning when I was very young, having stayed the night at a family friend's home, I remember the family of five plus me were all tucked up in their parents' bed. One of the children asked her mum, who was sitting at the end of the bed, what the difference was between them and me, as I was adopted. I immediately felt uncomfortable and didn't know where to look. Without hesitation, though, she said to all of us: 'Well, unfortunately we had no choice having each of you, but Gay and Kathleen chose Suzy and Crona, so that makes them extra special.' That's all she had to say. How easy it can be to make a child feel special.

This letter also personally chimed with my own experience of adoption.

> Dear Gay,
> At first, I wanted to take Hugh Leonard and shake him
> till his teeth rattled; but then I thought: No, his
> opinion was formed by his experience, and that's sad. My

experience, I suppose, has formed my opinion, but _it_ is happy. What made me cross was Hugh Leonard saying that, in his opinion, adoption must always have a bad effect on the child, and that it is better to be brought up by one person of 'your own' than by two people unrelated to you. I think it is the love and concern that matters even more than the relatedness.

In our family we have children who are adopted and children who are born to us; and I simply cannot see any difference in my heart between the two. I love my eldest son just as fiercely and with as much pride as my youngest daughter, and the ones in between make me laugh one minute and despair the next in fairly equal proportions.

And certainly, I feel that to give a child for adoption signifies love on the mother's part; it takes great love to give away your baby from your own care, knowing that you will always wonder is she all right, knowing you will feel guilty, knowing she may blame you. But twenty years ago the problems of how to work and look after a baby, and the financial impossibility of looking after it without work, were insurmountable; and many a mother opted for putting her baby into a home where she felt he would be wanted and therefore loved, financially secure, and likely to be educated; where he would be part of a 'normal' family, not a stigmatised outcast, even though it tore her to pieces for years and years to come. Yes, I think that showed love. And I thank her for her trust in me, and hope I have been worthy of her trust.

Hugh Leonard. Mon 6ᵗʰ Oct.
Re.

Dear Gay,

At first I wanted to take Hugh Leonard
& shake him till his teeth rattled; but
then I thought — No, his opinion was
formed by his experience, and that's
sad. My experience, I suppose, has
formed my opinion, but it is happy.
What made me cross was Hugh
Leonard saying that in his opinion
adoption must always have a bad
effect on the child, and that it is
better to be brought up by one person
of "your own" than by two people
unrelated to you. I think it is the
love and concern, that matters even
more, than the relatedness.
In our family we have children
who are adopted and children who
are born to us; and I simply cannot
see any difference in my heart
between the two. I love my eldest
son just as fiercely and with as much

Here is another response from someone who had been adopted as a child.

I'm adopted myself. I don't agree at all with what the man is saying. He must be very mixed up himself and must have had an unhappy childhood. I would love to thank my natural mother for giving me up for adoption and for giving me an opportunity in life. I'm in the process of adopting at the moment myself, having gone through infertility problems. I feel what the man has said will upset girls who have given up their babies for adoption, will upset adoptive parents and those who are themselves adopted. I certainly thank my natural mother for giving me up and giving me two wonderful parents.

And then there are the letters from mothers. This one stood out for me.

My blood is boiling listening to Hugh Leonard. I had a baby when I was 19, back in 1970. I gave him up for adoption. I wasn't afraid at the time. I was only nineteen and in that emotional state you would just do what people tell you to do. If I'd kept my baby I know he'd have gone through hell. Thousands of people have no children of their own and would love to adopt a baby and could probably give them a much better life and opportunity in life than I could have given my child. I did leave my name with the home I was in on the Navan Road, just in case my son ever wants to contact me. I've gone through both situations, having to give up my child for adoption, and also I've not been able to have children, although I have now.

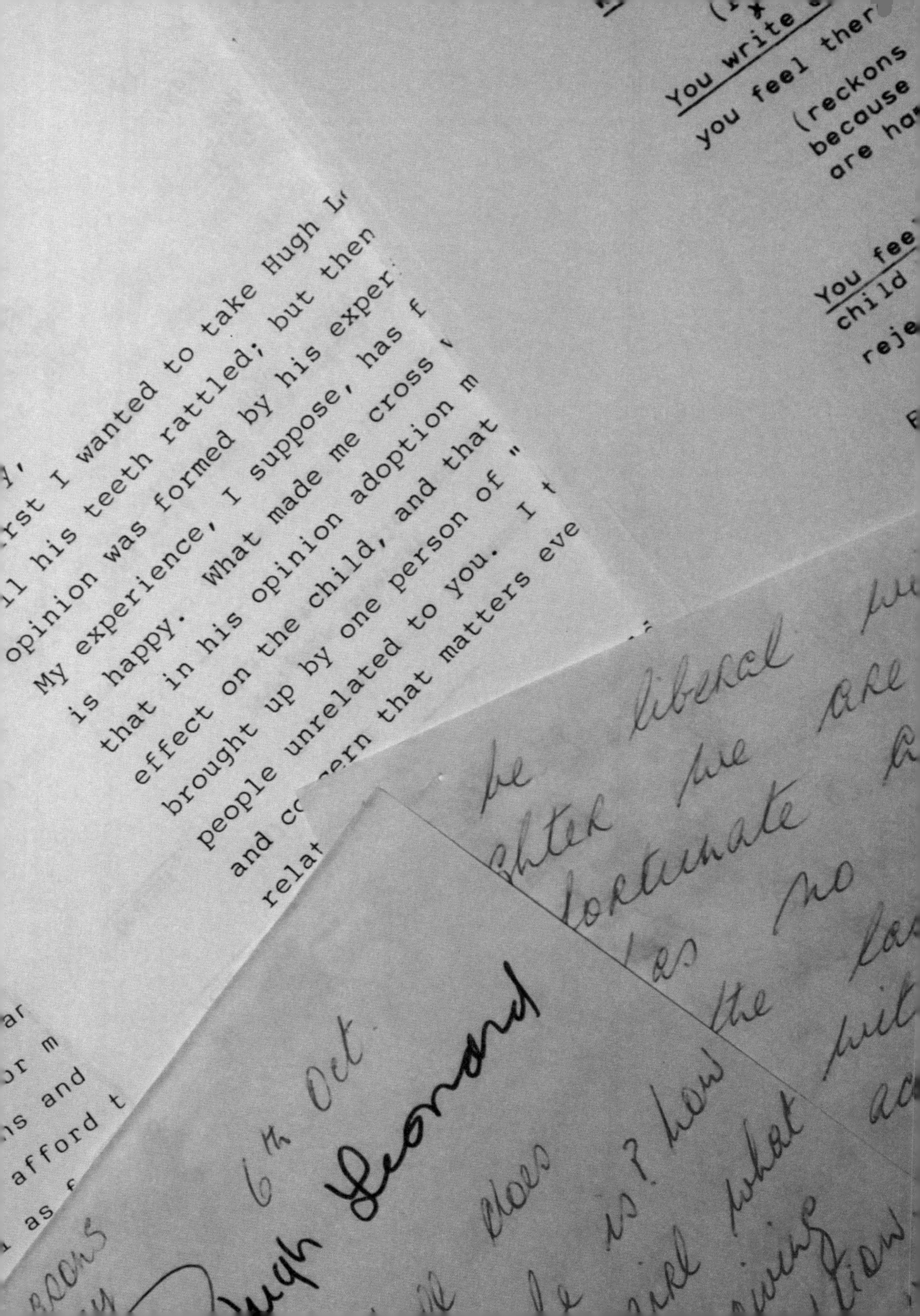

You write s
you feel ther

(reckons
because
are ha

You fee
child
reje

y,
rst I wanted to take Hugh L
ll his teeth rattled; but then
opinion was formed by his exper
My experience, I suppose, has f
is happy. What made me cross
that in his opinion adoption m
effect on the child, and that
brought up by one person of "
people unrelated to you. I t
and co ern that matters eve
relat

ar
or m
s and
afford t
as

be liberal
ghter he are
fortunate
as no
does how the la
6th Oct. e is? how it

Hugh Leonard
nal what

As with so many of the subjects aired on *The Gay Byrne Show*, listeners often disagreed with each other, or offered a different perspective on the matter under discussion. A topic such as adoption, which Gay knew affected the homes of listeners the length and breadth of Ireland, is a clear example. It was vitally important to Gay that the letters, all of which exposed the harsh reality of life rather than the accepted image of Ireland promoted by the authorities and the Church, be given air time. Here's another letter that stood out, this time from a young, unmarried mother who made the decision to keep her baby:

Dear Gay,

I am a girl of 21. I live in a small town in the country. When I was 18 years old, I had a beautiful baby girl. While I was pregnant my boyfriend (as he was then) and I moved to a flat in Dublin. Nobody in my hometown knew I was expecting. They thought I had a job. We had decided to give our baby for adoption. My parents came to see us all the time (my parents knew) in Dublin but put no pressure on us one way or the other, with regard to marriage or adoption.

But to finish, we kept the baby and married later. Our marriage is a happy one.

But Hugh Leonard said that he knew girls who kept their babies and had no regrets. I do have regrets about keeping her. My husband had and still has no work. She is fed well but she has no new clothes or shoes or anything that would make life good for her. I feel if I had given her up, she would have gotten so much more than I can give her. Christmas is coming and I am searching second-hand shops for Santa. Don't get me wrong, my husband and I love her very much, but we can't help feeling that our selfishness has done her wrong. It would have been easier to give her up because it was hard to get released from hospital with my own baby. They put tremendous pressure on me to give up my baby. They kept me in three days extra.

What struck me about this particular batch of letters and stories was that each letter and each story shed new light on a different aspect of the same subject. Today, because of social media algorithms, conversations like this one often fracture into different echo chambers – but in 1986 there were very few places a conversation like this could happen, and one of those places was *The Gay Byrne Show*. It is fascinating to turn the pages of the show files and discover another letter, another story, another perspective.

In 1987, news broke of a baby girl who had been found abandoned at Saint Joseph's Catholic Church on Berkeley Road in north Dublin and taken to the Rotunda Hospital for treatment. A few days later, Gay had an update for his listeners: baby Emma, as she had been named, was healthy and being looked after, but George Henry, Master of the Rotunda Hospital, had received this letter, supposedly from the baby's mother.

Dear Dr Henry,
You don't know me but I am the mother of little baby Emma. Please take care of her and find her good parents that can take good care of her. I gave her up because I could never be able to take care of her. I work during the day and no one knew that I was pregnant and it would not be accepted where I come from.
    I beg of you to find proper parents for little Emma that can give her anything she wants and needs as I could never afford to do this. Giving Emma up was hard but it is something I will have to live with. It's better this way and I'll always love her and miss her.
    Thanking you,
    Little Emma's mother

Gay explained the situation: 'Emma can't be placed with proper parents, can't be put up for adoption under the existing laws, without her mother's consent. So, please, please, Emma's mother, if you're listening to this, get in touch with Dr Henry at the Rotunda Hospital. You will be dealt with in the utmost confidentiality but they

The Gay Byrne Show:

7th — 11th Sept. '87.

must have your signature, your permission, in order to find Emma the parents and home you want for her.'

Baby Emma's mother's letter perfectly illustrates the kind of society we lived in in those years: conservative, shame-ridden, judgemental, Catholic yet often deeply unchristian.

But change was slow. Three years had passed since the death of Ann Lovett and her baby son. Despite all the national hand-wringing and determination that this could not happen again, baby Emma's mother still felt that she had nobody to whom she could turn and had to face her pregnancy alone.

In any circumstances, adoption is not something that's entered into lightly: for either those giving up their child for adoption or for those deciding to adopt a child. While the full story of adoption in Ireland – the abuse and injustices suffered by so many – was yet to unfold, what we see in these letters are the first ripples of what would later lead to a tidal wave of change. Discontent is quietly bubbling beneath the surface of these letters. The people were beginning to find their voice. But in 1992, one letter would lead to an interview on the show which shocked the nation and unveiled one of Ireland's most horrific scandals: the systematic abuse of children in Ireland's industrial schools.

6

The Christine Buckley Story

—

ON 13 NOVEMBER 1992, *The Late Late Show* ran a special anniversary show to mark 400 years since the founding of Trinity College Dublin. As was Gay's style, he went into the audience that night to speak to those in attendance. In the audience sat a Nigerian doctor named Ariwodo Kalunta, and Gay wanted to speak to him. Gay told the audience that Kalunta was an old family friend. He had been at Trinity with Gay's brother Al and he had regularly visited the Byrne family home on the South Circular Road. Gay's mother had been very fond of Kalunta, and he of her – particularly her chips, he said, which were legendary. Kalunta told Gay that it had been 40 years since he was last in Dublin. The reason for his visit this time, he said, was to be reunited with his daughter. His daughter sat beside him that evening in *The Late Late Show* audience. At this point, Gay knew nothing of the story behind the reunion of father and daughter.

A few days later, Gay received a letter from a woman named Christine Buckley. In her letter, Christine explained to Gay that she had spent her childhood in an orphanage, St Vincent's Industrial School, Goldenbridge, popularly known as Goldenbridge, and how, 40 years later, she had struggled to find her mother and, later, her father. To add authenticity and get his full attention, she ended her letter: 'My father is Ariwodo Kalunta.'

Her principal reason for telling her story to Gay was to spur on others like her who might want to find out about their own parents. As a result of the letter, Gay invited both Christine and Ariwodo onto the radio programme to share their story. The resulting interview would grip the country in a way previously unseen. They did not know it at the time, but that interview would lift the lid on one of Ireland's darkest and most shameful chapters, one whose horrors would dominate headlines for decades to come.

The story that Christine came into the studio to tell was initially about the difficulty she faced in trying to trace her parents: the wall of obstacles that the system put in her way, administrative requirements she had to work through, and misinformation she was fed. However, it was her description of life in the orphanage – one of constant beatings, mental abuse, sadistic cruelty, unending tedious work – that caught listeners' attention. With remarkable calm and clarity, Christine recounted what she had experienced at Goldenbridge from the age of four to seventeen. Each child was given a number and was referred to as that number rather than their own names: Christine was number 89. She experienced horrific beatings at the hands of nuns, on one occasion being hospitalised and requiring stiches. Upon entering hospital, she was warned not to tell hospital staff how she had sustained these injuries – to say, instead, that she had fallen. Christine and the other girls at the orphanage, she said, were forced to work every day – stringing rosary beads – and if they didn't hit their daily quotas they were flogged.

Christine's interview started at 10 a.m., and by 10.20 a.m. the switchboard in RTÉ was jammed. Christine herself had absolutely no idea at that point that there were so many other institutions across the country, and countless other people who had gone through exactly the same abuse that she had. Letters and phone calls from survivors flooded into the show. The media immediately took up the story, uncovering more and more horrors. But it was Mary Raftery's 1999 documentary series *States of Fear* that finally exposed the extent of the abuse suffered by children in institutional care in Ireland. Before the final episode aired, then Taoiseach Bertie Ahern apologised on behalf of the state to victims like Christine and countless others, 'for our collective failure to intervene, to detect their pain, to come to their rescue.'

The letters I have included here are just a handful of what was sent to Gay in the days and weeks following Christine's interview. Some of the letters come from women who knew Christine personally, having been at Goldenbridge with her, corroborating her story and adding their own shocking accounts of abuse and deprivation. Others come from people who suffered similar abuse but in different institutions. Many of the letters are from people who had never before uttered a word about their own harrowing experiences. Christine, taking a stand and speaking publicly on this subject, gave other people the courage to follow her lead and finally expose what had been whispered about and quietly ignored for decades.

Fi

CHRISTINE BUCKLEY

INTRO

THERE ARE STORIES AND THERE ARE STORIES.....WE HEAR A LOT OF THEM
HERE ON THE GAY BYRNE SHOW.....WELL, I HAVE A STORY THIS MORNING
WHICH IS UP THERE WITH THE BEST OF THEM.....IT IS THE TRUE STORY OF
ONE IRISH WOMANS LIFE TO DATE AND THAT WOMAN IS CHRISTINE BUCKLEY
- SITTING ACROSS FROM ME IS CHRISTINE AND THE FIRST THING THAT YOU
WOULD NOTICE ABOUT CHRISTINE - IF YOU WERE HERE IN THE STUDIO WITH
ME....IS THAT SHE IS BLACK ....OR COLOURED.....OR NON WHITE
CAUCASIAN OR WHATEVER YOU WANT TO SAY YOURSELF....AND I AM ONLY
TELLING YOU THAT BECAUSE IT IS RELEVANT TO THE STORY...

CHRISTINE - YOU WERE BORN IN 1946 AND YOU ENDED UP AFTER A LOT OF
TOOING AND FROOING, IN AN ORPHANAGE AT THE AGE OF 4 ....DID YOU
HAVE ANY IDEA WHO YOUR PARENTS WERE ?

- SHE REMEMBERED A TALL BLACK MAN AND A FRIENDLY ~~BLONDE~~ *Red haired* WOMAN WHO
USED TO VISIT HER VERY EARLY ON.......SHE HAD BEEN FOSTERED FOR A
SHORT WHILE OUT TO A SMALL TOWN OUTSIDE DUBLIN BUT WAS TOLD THAT
SHE WOULD HAVE TO LEAVE THERE BECAUSE THE LOCAL CLERGY SAID THAT "
THERE WAS NO WAY A LITTLE BLACK GIRL COULD GO TO THE VILLAGE
SCHOOL"....SO SHE WAS PACKED OFF AND ENDED UP IN THE ORPHANAGE....

* THE ORHPANAGE THEN - IT IS CLOSED DOWN NOW BUT WHEN YOU WERE
THERE HOW MANY OTHER CHILDREN WERE THERE AS WELL ?

SOMETIMES *seemed to be hundreds* ~~HUNDREDS~~ IN THE PLACE......ALL AGES....

* AND WHAT WERE THE CONDITIONS LIKE?

- PRIMITIVE....COLD....BAD FOOD....CONTROL THROUGH TERROR

* THE NUNS IN CHARGE WERE VERY STRICT ?

- VERY BAD STORIES OF THE CRUELTY....MINDLESS STUFF....IF YOU
SLEPT IN THE WRONG POSITION - I.E. WITH YOUR HANDS ANYWHERE EXCEPT
CROSSED OVER YOUR CHEST WITH THE ROSARY BEADS WRAPPED AROUND
THEM....YOU WOULD BE WOKEN UP WITH THE SLAP OF A BELT....MANY
OTHER PUNISHMENTS BASED ON STANDING FOR HOURS WITHOUT FALLING
ASLEEP OR ELSE FACING THE LEATHER....OTHER DEGRADATIONS -
PARTICULARLY FOR YOUNG GIRLS GROWING UP.....

* DID YOU EVER THINK THAT THERE WAS A RACIST ELEMENT IN THEIR
TREATMENT - WERE YOU SINGLED OUT ?

- SHE WAS ALWAYS WILFUL.....ALWAYS HAD INDEPENDENT STREAK.....SHE
SNEAKED OUT A LETTER TO ONE OF THE NATIONAL NEWPAPERS WITH THE
~~BREAD~~ MAN....IT WAS PUBLISHED....SHE DIDNT SIGN IT BUT SHE DID
NAME THE ORPHANAGE.......THERE WAS HELL..... EVERY SINGLE CHILD
FROM AGED 5 UPWARDS WAS BROUGHT INTO THE YARD AND ONE NUN BEGAN TO
SYSTEMATICALLY HIT THE CHILDREN ON THE LEGS UNTIL SOMEONE OWNED
UP...SHE BROKE......MAJOR PUNISHMENTS.....

Notes for Gay's interview with Christine in November 1992.

* EVENTUALLY THOUGH - YOU DID GET HIS NAME - WHO WAS HE AND WHERE
WAS HE ?

ARiwodo [aRRi-Nood 4]

- HIS NAME TURNED OUT TO BE KALUNTA AND HE IS A PSYCHIATRIST WITH
HIS OWN HOSPITAL IN NIGERIA.

* AND FINALLY - AFTER YOU WENT THROUGH A LOT OF TOOING AND
FROOING, HE WROTE TO YOU AND YOU STARTED CORRESPONDING - TELL ME
ABOUT WHEN YOU DECIDED TO GO AND SEE HIM ?

- IT WAS 1986 WHEN THEY GOT IN TOUCH AND SHE WAS WRITING EVERY
WEEK AND HE WASNT.......EVENTUALLY SHE GOT TIRED OF THE WHOLE
THINGS AND DECIDED TO VISIT HIM. IN.. Feb. 1988.

* WAS HE KEEN - DID HE HAVE HIS OWN FAMILY OUT THERE ?

- HE WAS MARRIED WITH 11 OTHER CHILDREN - (██████████████
████████████████)......

* SO YOU BOUGHT THE TICKET - TELL ME WHAT HAPPENED FROM THEN ON ?

3 DAYS BEFORE DEPARTURE.....TICKETS BOUGHT ETC.....TELEGRAM
ARRIVED SAYING " *DEFER VISIT. EXPLANATORY LETTER TO FOLLOW*".
SHE WAS DISTRAUGHT...WENT TO BED FOR A FULL DAY AND NIGHT.....WOKE
UP AND KNEW WHAT TO DO.....SENT A LETTER SAYING " *HAVE IGNORED
TELEGRAM.....AM ON MY WAY.*"

* AND YOU ARRIVED IN THE HOTEL WHERE YOU WERE SUPPOSED TO MEET
HIM.......YOU WERE WITH A GIRLFRIEND......AND YOU WERE WAITING AT
RECEPTION...

- THEY WAITED FOR 3 HOURS....EVERY BLACK MAN - AND THEY WERE ALL
BLACK....WHO CAME THROUGH THE DOOR WAS POTENTIALLY HER
FATHER....SHE WAS SO NERVOUS....EVENTUALLY REALSIED THAT HE WASNT
COMING....SHE WAS SO UPSET.....LEFT A MESSAGE SAYING WHERE THEY
WERE AND WENT DOWN THE ROAD TO A RESTAURANT.......AN HOUR AND A
HALF LATER WHEN SHE HAD STOPPED LOOKING AROUND, MARY SAID " HERE
HE IS"   AND A MAN ARRIVED...PUT HIS HANDS ON HER SHOULDERS AND
SAID " HELLO CHRISTINE".......SHE TURNED AROUND.....AND LET RIP
WITH ALL THE VENOM SHE COULD MUSTER...GAVE HIM WHAT
FOR....TOLD HIM OFF....EVERYTHING SHE HAD BEEN BUILDING UP INSIDE
HER.....SHE NOTICED A WOMAN STANDING BESIDE HIM - HIS WIFE BUT
DIDNT REALLY TAKE HIM IN OR ANYTHING...... EVENTUALLY THEY ALL SAT
DOWN AND DRANK CHAMPAGNE....THERE WERE A FEW MORE STRESSFUL
MOMENTS BUT BY THE END OF THE TRIP THEY WERE BEST OF FRIENDS AND
HE INTRODUCED HER ALL AROUND AS HIS DAUGHTER ETC.

* WELL DR KALUNTA IS ALSO HERE THIS MORNING - HE ARRIVED HER LAST
WEEK ON HIS FIRST VISIT BACK TO IRELAND IN FORTY ODD YEARS
....FIRST TIME TO SEE YOUR THREE GRANDCHILDREN.........FILL ME IN
A BIT ON YOUR LIFE

* YOU STUDIED MEDICINE IN TRINITY THEN AND WHAT AGE WERE YOU WHEN
CHRISTINE WAS BORN

██
██

* AND AT ALL TIMES - DID YOU KEEP SOME PICTURE ALIVE OF A MOTHER
AND A FATHER BEING SOMEWHERE OUT THERE FOR YOU ?

- A LOVELY DUBLIN WOMAN WHOM SHE CALLED MAMMY MARTIN DID VISIT HER
AND S T ADOPTED HER AS A SORT OF SURROGATE...PRETENDED TO OTHERS
THAT HE WAS HER MUM ETC.....

* AND YOU GOT OUT THEN TO GO TO SCHOOL - AND YOU DID WELL AT
SCHOOL ?

- THERE WERE JUST 3 OF THE ORPHANAGE GIRLS ALLOWED OUT AND THEY
HAD A HARD TIME WHEN THEY CAME BACK BECAUSE THEY ABSOLUTLEY HAD TO
MAKE 60 PAIRS OF ROSARY BEADS EVERY SINGLE AFTERNOON WHEN THEY
CAME HOME FROM SCHOOL.....NO TIME FOR STUDY.

- EVENTUALLY IT GOT SORTED OUT AND THEY GOT TO STUDY....SHE DID
HER LEAVING.

* LETS SKIP ON OVER THE NEXT FEW YEARS, CHRISTINE.....YOU
EVENTUALLLY BECAME A NURSE AND YOU GOT MARRIED TO DONAL AND YOU
HAD THREE LOVELY CHILDREN AND THEN YOU WERE SUDDENLY 39 YEARS OF
AGE AND YOU DECIDED TO FIND YOUR REAL PARENTS

* WHY DID YOU FEEL THAT THE TIME HAD COME ?
- ACTUALLY SHE HAD BEEN SICK AFTER THE BIRTH OF HER THIRD CHILD
AND SHE HAD A HYSTERECTOMY AND GENERALLY FELT NOT
GREAT.....DECIDED ON NEW YEARS EVE......THIS YEAR IS GOING TO BE
THE YEAR......SET HERSELF THE CHALLENGE AND THREW HERSELF INTO
IT....

* AND YOU STARTED THE HUNT THEN.......I PRESUME YOU WENT THE
USUAL PLACES, BIRTHS, MARRIAGES AND DEATHS AND ALL THAT SORT OF
THING......AND YOU FINALLY TRACKED DOWN YOUR MOTHER......I KNOW
YOU DONT WANT TO IDENTIFY HER BECAUSE THERE ARE OTHER
COMPLICATIONS BUT TELL ME ABOUT MEETING HER FOR THE FIRST TIME ?

- SHE DESCRIBES MEETING HER MOTHER AS BEING A LITTLE BIT LIKE A
BEREAVEMENT.....BASICALLY SHE WAS NOT AS SHE EXPECTED - THE IMAGE
IN HER MIND WAS ACTUALLY OF THE WOMAN WHO HAD BEEN WITH HER FATHER
AND THIS WAS ACTUALLY HIS LANDLADY WHO JUST TOOK AN INTEREST, SO
SHE HAD THE WRONG IMAGE IN HER HEAD......
   ...HER MOTHER WAS ABOUT 70 ......WHEN CHRISTINE WALKED INTO THIS
BIG ROOM AND SAW HER SITTING ON A CHAIR SHE FELT NOTHING.....NO
SENSE OF DISCOVERY....NO EMOTION....THE WOMAN SAT THERE AND WAS A
STRANGER.

* EVENTUALLY THOUGH DID YOU BREAK THROUGH THAT AND BECOME FRIENDS
?

- YES BUT THERE IS STILL A BIT OF STRAIN

* AND YOU DECIDED THEN THAT YOU ABSOLUTLEY HAD TO FIND YOUR
FATHER......YOUR MOTHER WOULDNT TALK ABOUT HIM AND YOU ONLY KNEW
THAT HE WAS BLACK.....WHERE DID YOU GO FROM THERE ?

- FIRST SHE FOUND OUT THAT HE HAD BEEN IN TRINITY......USING THE
SURNAME SHE *THOUGHT* WAS HIS SHE FOUND OUT THE NAMES OF ALL THE
STUDENTS IN TRINITY DURING THE RELEVANT TIME . THERE WERE ONLY
3 NINE OF THEM. SHE RANG THEM ALL.......THE LAST ONE SHE RANG SAID
" JESUS MARY AND JOSEPH - I ALWAYS KNEW THIS PHONE CALL WOULD
COME...I HAD A DAUGHTER AND I HAVE WONDERED ALL THIS YEARS WHERE
YOU WERE "   CHRISTINE WAS SO EXCITED AND ONLY AT THE END OF THE
CALL DID SHE REMEMBER TO SAY " I FORGOT TO SAY....YOU ARE BLACK
ARENT YOU...????? ".....HE SAID " OH NO,MY DEAR , I AM
WHITE...".....WRONG GUY.....OBVIOUSLY OTHER STUDENTS AT THE TIME
WERE FATHERING DAUGHTERS AND NEVER SEEING THEM AGAIN...!!!

Following publication of the Ryan report in 2009, when asked what her reaction was to being finally vindicated, Christine made an emotional plea. 'Listen to children, believe them when they say something has happened.' It may have taken too long for the truth to come out, but now that it had, Gay and his audience were ready to listen. The repercussions of these stories are still being felt in Ireland today.

Christine Buckley in 1996.

The day after Christine's interview, the RTÉ radio centre had received so many responses that Gay continued the story. 'We got a lot of calls yesterday', Gay says, 'about Christine and her extraordinary story. Many, many people who rang us to say how upset they had been or how much the story touched them. And a number of people who knew Christine and who had been with her in the orphanage wanted to get back in touch. Quite a number of callers ... rang to ask if anyone is answerable for the sort of misery and mistreatment that she went through. One caller said: "Wouldn't it be nice if the nuns simply said, 'We are sorry ... We got it wrong'?". Another caller asked: "Is there anyone to answer for the treatment – surely someone has to explain their behaviour."' It would be some time before anything close to an answer – or an apology – was received.

A woman who was also at Goldenbridge and who knew Christine wrote:

Dear Gay,
I was also in Goldenbridge. I arrived there in September
1945, clutching my little sister's hand. First impressions

were of gates so high they seemed to reach into the very sky. A girl with a big bunch of keys opened the gates. I saw loads of big windows and what struck me then was that there were no curtains like we had at home - just huge bare windows.

Yes, it was hard. I remember a little two-and-a-half-year-old dying there, from falling off a bench. They were left to play on their own. A girl of my own age often had a bleeding ear from being slapped too hard.

At about 2 a.m. every night a teacher would drag all the little ones who might wet their beds out to go to the toilet. I saw some of these kids actually crawl under the beds to go back to sleep.

Us big girls could rob bread for our little sisters. The only drink of water we got was out of a toilet cistern. We would save the lid off Nugget polish to get the water. My mam was sick but my aunties were good to us and they would take us out every third Sunday of the month. That's how I'd have a polish lid.

We never, in the seven years I was there, tasted an egg or rasher. Four years after being there we started to get a sausage once a week. The big bully girls would make the little ones bring out their sausages up their sleeve for them to eat.

I could go on for ever … I knew Chrissie … We were all innocent victims.

The next letter comes from a woman who experienced similar abuse but in a different orphanage. Like Christine, she had attempted to locate her birth parents. The fact that not only had she been listening to the interview the day before, but the woman who helped her had also been listening illustrates the national forum for discussion that *The Gay Byrne Show* had become.

Hi Gay,

Listening to the girl on your show yesterday who was brought up in an orphanage brought back many memories for me.

Like her, I too was brought up in one. We were punished for normal things that children do. Beaten with wooden hangers, stripped and beaten with canes and leather straps for wetting the bed. Left in a room all night with just the floor to sleep on. No blankets, just your nighty. I could give you a list of what went on. Once I got my arm broken with the leg of a chair. They told the doctor I fell and I wasn't to say anything. It brought back so many memories I cried just remembering.

I've been looking for my parents. About a month ago I found out where my father is. About eight months ago I found out about my mother. Unfortunately, she died two years ago. I found out one of her daughter's married names. I rang all the names in the phone book in that area.

By luck one of the ladies I was talking to was very nice and did know my mother. Of course she didn't know who I was as I had told her I was a friend of that person. Anyway, after your show I was crying because I remembered my childhood and felt guilty about lying to this nice lady who was so nice. So I rang her and made a fool of myself by crying. I told her the truth, who I was, crying while telling her, and again she was very nice […].

Gay, if this lady is listening this morning, tell her thanks from me, sorry for making a fool of myself … I wish her all the happiness and the best for her family.

Along with people sharing their own stories, the letters started to ask how those involved – the religious orders who ran the schools and orphanages – would be investigated. It would take a few years of relentless campaigning until, finally,

Hi Gary,

Listening to the girl on your show yesterday who was brought up in an orphanage brought back many memories for me.

Like her, I too was brought up in one. We were punished for normal things that children do. Beaten with wooden hangers, stripped and beaten with canes and leather straps for wetting the bed. Left in a room all night with just the floor to sleep on. No blankets, just your nighty. I could give you a list of what went on. Once I got my arm broken with the leg of a chair. They told the doctor I fell and I wasn't to say anything. It brought back so many memories I cried just remembering.

I've been looking for my parents. About a month ago I found out where my father is. About eight months ago I found out about my mother. Unfortunately, she died two years ago. I found out one of her daughter's married names. I rang all the names in the phone book in that area.

By luck one of the ladies I was talking to was very nice and did know in May 1999 the Commission to Inquire into Child Abuse was set up. Its report, commonly referred to as the Ryan Report, was published ten years later, in 2009. It detailed abuse and neglect reported by over 1,000 men and women in over 200 institutional residences since 1914. It described children living in a 'climate of fear' within these settings, and revealed that the Department of Education had a 'deferential and submissive attitude' towards the orders that set up and ran them. On its publication, the *Irish Times* described it as a 'devastating indictment of Church and State authorities' and 'the map of an Irish hell'.

Back in 1992, only those who had been in these institutions knew the full extent of the horrors within those walls. But Christine's letter had opened the Pandora's Box, and the letters from survivors flooded in.

Dear Gay,

Congratulations on your interview with Christine on Wednesday morning. She sounded so beautiful and caring and she must be so resilient to have withstood such savagery. I would say there wasn't a woman in the country (and I hope many men also) whose blood didn't boil as she gave us the account of the savage treatment meted out to this innocent young life.

I spent two years in a boarding school from the age of nine to eleven years. My experiences were quite horrific, and I know that I carry the scars to this day. Like Christine, I'm very happily married with children. Because of my experiences, I wouldn't trust anybody with my children, so that I would not expose them to any cruelty. Thank God they've grown up to a mature adulthood with no fear and carrying the baggage of past horrors. No doubt Christine's children will benefit also.

As for these perpetrators who think they can hide behind their habits, I think that these institutions should be investigated immediately, as we hope another Christine will not sit in 20 years and give us a similar story.

I went into teaching myself and loved it. I think I went into the profession to protect the children who crossed my path of life. […] I would love to know that anyone who has anything to do with children was kept under close scrutiny - as what more could we give our children but to grow up without fear and a lot of love.

Thanks, again, Christine.

As For these perpetrators who think they can hide behind their habits, I think that these institutions should be investigated immediately, as we hope another Christine will not sit in 20 yrs and give us a similar story.

What was coming out on air at this time made difficult listening for everyone. The abuse that was now being revealed had long been hinted at, but as with many other difficult topics throughout Ireland's history, it was easier to sweep it under the rug. Some people were not ready to hear the truth – to face the reality of what had been going on behind closed doors for so long. In addition to the personal stories, Gay received letters, like this one, from people who, for whatever warped reasons, could not accept what they were hearing. Even though people were now speaking out, the shift in mindset was not instant.

Sir,

Regarding that lady that went to Africa to find her father. Her story was a fantastic one indeed. She was one that wasn't going to be beaten, headstrong, arrogant and unmanageable, etc. One can imagine what kind of child she was.

In those days the people that are now condemning the religious orders would not themselves have anything to do with illegitimate children, and they were right because they understood the dangers that illegitimacy would be to proper breeding of future generations. So there was no place for those illegitimate and deserted children except in the convents and monasteries.

In those days the religious orders themselves were under very strict rules, having very little time to attend to the progress of children that wanted to be spoiled.

The nuns were called to their religious exercises, to answer a bell five or six times a day, together with domestic work as each had to pull their weight for the community.

It isn't difficult to understand why nuns and brothers couldn't have time and patience to deal with all types of illegitimate and deserted children that the gamut of the people didn't want to know about.

As with all topics, Gay never censored opinion, or filtered listeners' responses. No opinion was off-limits, and many would provoke horrified reactions from listeners. This letter was no different. Many wrote in to the show after Gay read out the letter above to offer Christine their support.

Dear Gay,
Excuse foolscap. I am so furious that I haven't the time to go out and buy a proper notepad. I listened to Christine's story last Wednesday and since that I have hardly slept, and when I did, on Friday and Saturday, with the help of tranquillisers, because that's what I had to resort to, I wet the bed. Just as I did then back in Goldenbridge.

Today listening to some of the replies, from small-minded insular people, I couldn't take any more. Who do these people think they are? They were not there. Would they have survived that Nazi camp, because that's what it was, I dare say so.

Christine, or Chrissie, or no. 89, which was her number and which is the way I knew her best, had the courage to eventually speak out. I for one salute her. …

I can't stop crying. I hope to contact Chrissie, or no. 89, soon because, up to now, I have buried the past. The first thing I will do now is go for counselling. Again, Gay, I salute Christine and I wish her a fresh new start.

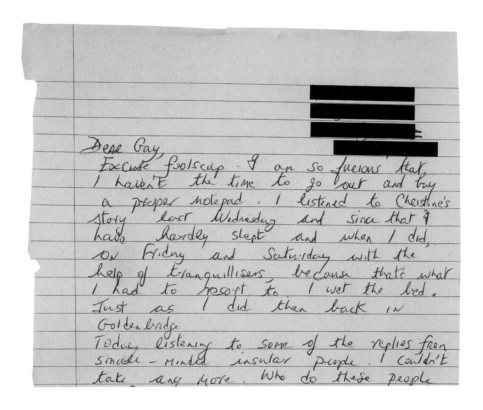

Dear Gay,
Excuse foolscap. I am so furious that I haven't the time to go out and buy a proper notepad. I listened to Christine's story last Wednesday and since that I have hardly slept and when I did, on Friday and Saturday with the help of tranquillisers, because that's what I had to resort to. I wet the bed. Just as I did then back in Goldenbridge.
Today listening to some of the replies from small-minded insular people. I couldn't take any more. Who do these people

...LED
...tells dad of
...phanage horror

● SMILES OF JOY: Christine and her dad are together again after her childhood ordeal in a Dublin orphanage run by nuns

...nter and father were reunited yesterday ...m the hell of a brutal orphanage ...naire's life in Nigeria.

...stened in rapt attention yesterday as abandoned ...uckley now 46 and a mother of three, told of her ...her medical student father Ariwodo Kalunta after a year.

...her story. ...exposed the ...child bashing ...which was ...Nuns.

...stine claimed that ...en were systemati-...beaten and psycho-...ically terrorised at the ...orphanage in Dublin.

The ...offences all hap-...pened in the 1950s, but at least one of the perpetra-tors is still alive, she said.

Suffering

In a graphic account of her suffering and that of her little children with her, Mrs Buckley described how.

"It was absolutely horrific. There were con-stant beatings. We were told continuously that we were sluts.

● "I was told my mother was a prostitute and my father a black good-for-nothing," black

● "Children as young as eight had to thread rosa-nes a day, until their thumbs and fingers were raw and covered with ... was beaten around for coming first

Christine says she was beaten, called a black good for nothing and forced to thread rosary beads

By SENAN MOLONY

in Christian Doctrine and called a little black bas-tard."

Mrs Buckley said that when couples came as prospective adoptive parents, she was pushed to the back and told: "You get back, no-one wants a black one."

When she wrote to a newspaper — through a letter smuggled via a breadman — about the cruelty at the home, all 250 children were lined up and threatened.

She admitted writing the letter and was beaten with a long, thick stick.

Christine was so badly injured that she was taken to hospital and 84 stitches inserted into the wounds.

She was made to say that the wounds were caused by a fall.

On one occasion when she went to stay with a family she was abused by the father.

Visits

A subsequent family who took her on visits treated her well, but she was beaten if she was smiling or wearing a nice coat when she returned.

Mrs Buckley was given up for adoption after she was fathered by a Nigerian who was study-ing medicine at a College. The ... visit her wa... ly told...

Dea...

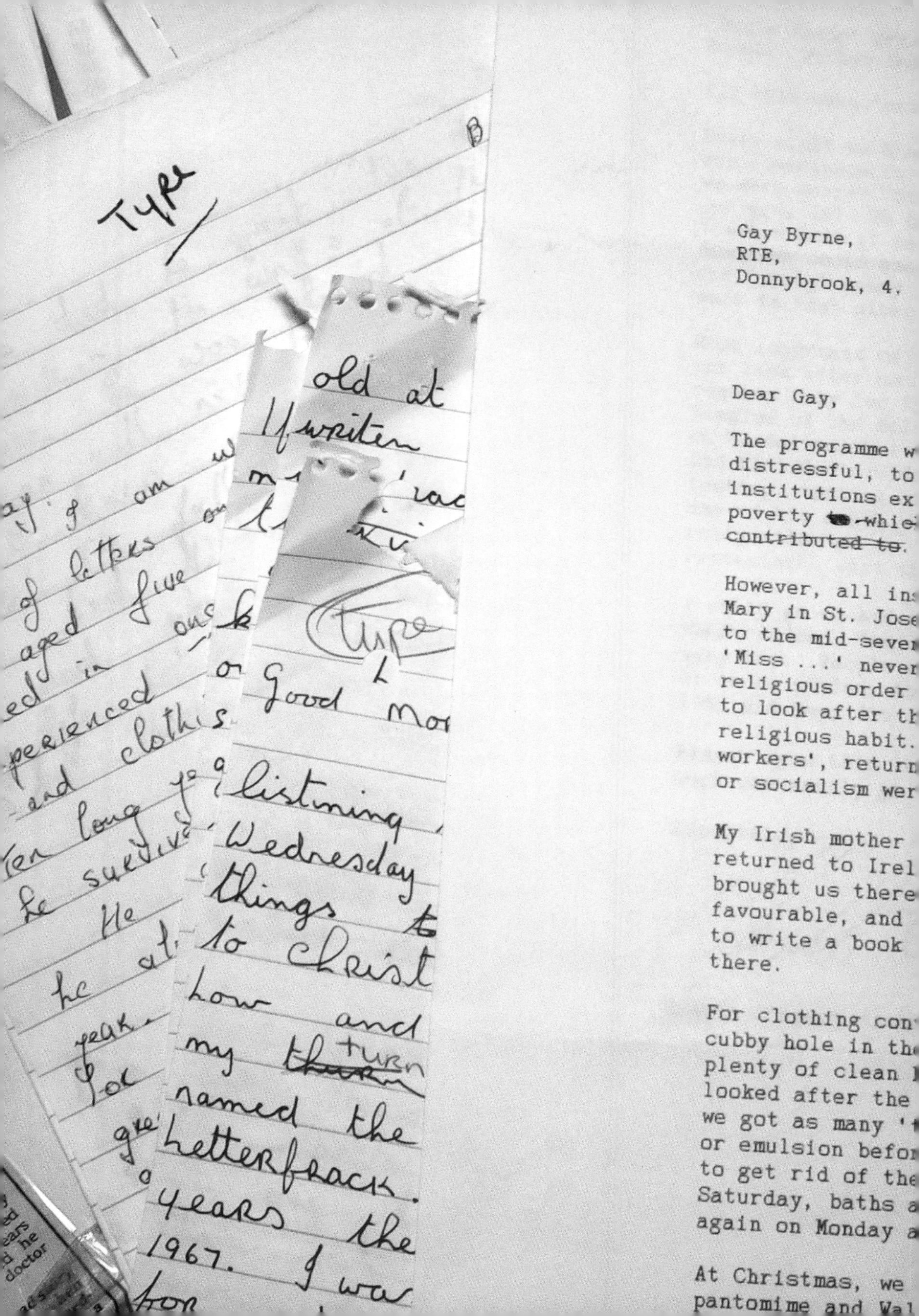

Handwritten note (top left):

Type /

B

Handwritten fragments (torn slips):

old at
If writer
m...'rac...
l...i...

...k
or Good Mo...

listining
Wednesday
things t...
to christ...
how   and
my turn t...
named the
Letterfrack.
Years the
1967. I wa...
for

...ay, I am w...
of letters on...
aged five
...ed in ou...
...perienced   ...
...and clothe...
Ten long t...
he survive...
He
he at...
...eak.
...or
...gre...

Typed letter (right side, partially visible):

Gay Byrne,
RTE,
Donnybrook, 4.

Dear Gay,

The programme w...
distressful, to...
institutions ex...
poverty ~~to which~~...
~~contributed to.~~

However, all ins...
Mary in St. Jose...
to the mid-seven...
'Miss ...' never...
religious order...
to look after th...
religious habit.
workers', return...
or socialism wer...

My Irish mother...
returned to Irel...
brought us there...
favourable, and...
to write a book...
there.

For clothing con...
cubby hole in the...
plenty of clean l...
looked after the...
we got as many 't...
or emulsion befor...
to get rid of the...
Saturday, baths a...
again on Monday a...

At Christmas, we...
pantomime and Wal...

As the letters and personal testimonies poured in, it became clear that this abuse had been going on for decades. They describe the long-lasting trauma the writers endured: the mental and physical scars they carried throughout their lives, and the lasting impact that this had on later generations of families.

Dear Gay,

I am writing in connection with your recent spate of letters on industrial schools. My father at the age of 5 years was orphaned and found himself placed in one of these cruel regimes. Here he experienced terrible physical abuse, deprivation in food and clothing with the strictest discipline and cruelty. Ten long years passed of this harsh treatment, which he somehow survived.

He married, had a family, became independent, but he always carried the inner scars of those terrible years. Damage resulted, he found himself with a hatred for all religions and all their practices. This caused great conflict within the home as my mother had a beautiful simple religion.

Christmas was such a miserable time. I can say it is one of my saddest memories. All religious events caused problems because he took no part in them, i.e. communions and confirmations. He was very strict. As we reached the age of nine or ten years, we would have to work from the time we arrived home from school. There was no time for play and this lasted until we got married, so my older brother and I missed out on what should have been happy years. Education was cut short and we were not allowed reach our full potential. It was like he was repeating with us all that he was deprived of. So you see, Gay, it does not stop when they leave those schools - there is a knock-on effect.

Before he died, he spent two days telling me of his life within the walls of the school and about where he was placed to learn a trade. I will never, ever forget his horrific story. I knew a little of his life at 12 years of age, but not the full story until he was on his dying bed. When he died, I stood by the bed and pleaded with him to let me go, as all my life he was in charge.

I don't blame him, but those so-called Christians!

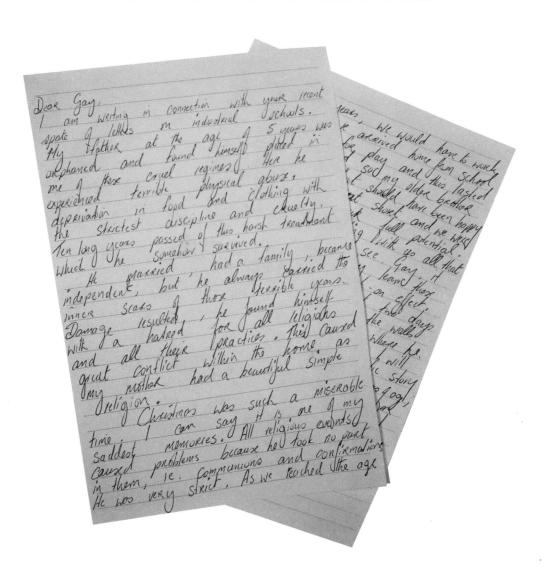

In December 1992, Hannah Mai Hutchinson wrote to Gay to tell her story. She was interviewed by Gay in the studio in January 1993, under the name Josephine, which was the name that had been given to her in 1963 by the nuns at Sean Ross Abbey Mother and Baby Home in Roscrea, County Tipperary. At 16 years of age, she became pregnant. She didn't know what pregnancy was. She thought one had to be married to have a baby. Banished by her parents when she was seven months pregnant, she went to Sean Ross Abbey. In her interview with Gay, she tells harrowing stories of her time there: one was of a 14-year-old girl, pregnant with twins, thrown out by her parents, who died alone in childbirth at the home; and of another girl, pregnant by her brother, abandoned by her parents.

Four months after giving birth, Hannah Mai was put on a train from Roscrea to Dublin with her son and a piece of paper on which was written the address of the Catholic Protection Society of Ireland. She was 16 years old and forced to give her baby up for adoption. She told Gay that, on handing over her son, having had him with her for four months, she was told to 'kiss your baby goodbye, you'll never see him again'. After her interview with Gay, Hannah Mai was contacted by a person who heard her and offered to help find her son. She did and, 30 years after losing him, they were reunited.

With these stories coming out, the letters that Gay had received some ten years earlier – with their descriptions of unloving, unsupportive families more concerned about the opinions of judgemental neighbours, and references to not having any choice but to put their babies up for adoption – read with new clarity. These systemic injustices had been going on for decades.

Dear Gay,
While I was listening to your programme [...] I was in despair because I thought I was pregnant. Why? Because I am unmarried and cannot get married at the moment. I am not a young teenager. I am nearly thirty, but still I could not bear what was to be ahead of me because of people's attitude, especially my parents.

I was physically sick at the very thought of telling them. My father once said to me that he would rather see me dead than see me pregnant. My mother was horrified the other night when I said I was going to see a young unmarried mother. She said to me to keep away from her, you don't need to associate with the likes of her. My parents are always praying and going to church and when I listen to them saying the rosary every night, I wonder, does God think like I do: that they have double standards?

Please, parents of Ireland, try and be more tolerant. The sexual act can happen in a matter of a few moments and is usually, like in my case, unplanned. When you are young and in love it is very hard to have control of your feelings all the time. Thank God I am not pregnant, but my heart aches for those poor girls who are not so lucky.

Parents of Ireland, try and be more tolerant. Look at all the violence and cruelty in the world. Surely the birth of a baby to an unmarried mother is not unforgiveable. Every baby is God's gift and not something to be ashamed of. Give your daughter and her baby all the love and support you can. It is better than all the rosaries in the world.

Within the discourse – the various points of view, differing opinions and heated arguments – these are very real women suffering, women who had very little support and were given little choice.

Dear Gay,
On listening to those letters this morning, they brought tears of my own memories being also an unmarried mother. I am not going into details, but the baby was adopted and I would like to say to you (who have two adopted children yourselves) and to the parents of adopted children lucky enough to have good homes, and parents who love their

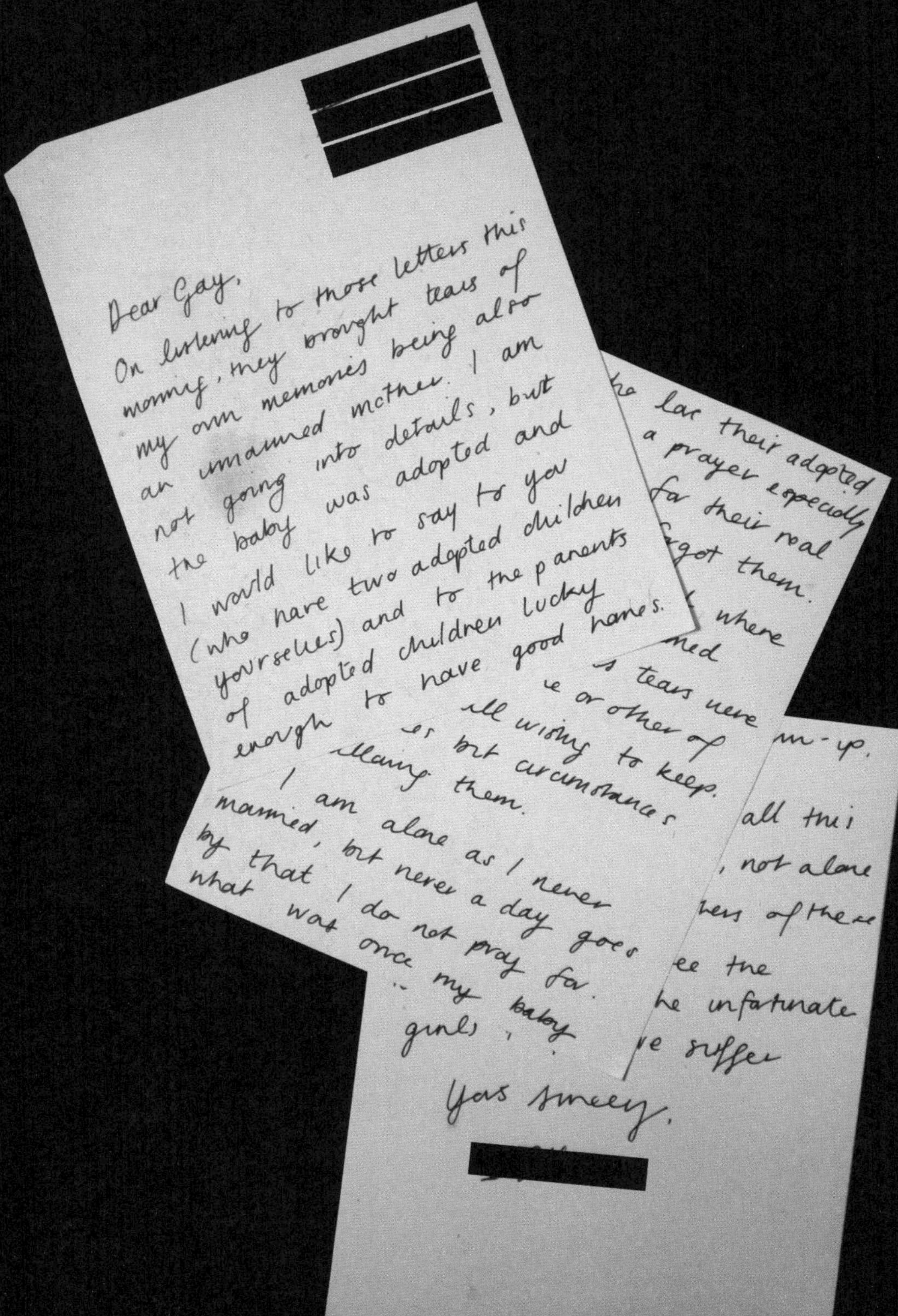

Dear Gay,

On listening to those letters this
morning, they brought tears of
my own memories being also
an unmarried mother. I am
not going into details, but
the baby was adopted and
I would like to say to you
(who have two adopted children
yourselves) and to the parents
of adopted children lucky
enough to have good homes.

... ke lar their adopted
... a prayer especially
... fa their real
... got them.
... where
... med
... tears were
... e or other of ... m-up.
... ll wrong to keep.
... es but circumstances ... all this
... llang them. ... , not alone
I am alone as I never ... hers of these
married, but never a day goes ... ee the
by that I do not pray for ... he infatuate
what I do ... my baby ... re suffer
... girls ...

Yas sincely.

adopted children, to say a prayer, especially on their birthdays, for their real mothers who never forget them.

The home in England where I had my baby was named Heartbreak Hotel, as tears were shed daily by one or other of the mothers, all wishing to keep their babies but circumstances not allowing them.

I am alone as I never married, but never a day goes by that I do not pray for what once was my baby, though now is a grown-up boy. As you say, I hope all this will be a lesson to, not alone parents, but the fathers of these babies who never see the heartbreak of the unfortunate girls they leave suffer.

Neither Christine Buckley nor Gay realised it the day they first spoke in the RTÉ Radio studio in 1992, but that interview would open one of the darkest chapters in Irish history. The repercussions of what they unwittingly uncovered that day are still unfolding decades on. As Nell McCafferty said, 'Gay was simply the right man in the right place at the right time.' And the letters and notes of listeners' phone calls are a compelling portrait of an Ireland divided: one part ready for change, the other afraid to let go of old certainties.

As with many of the subjects that Gay tackled, he would never accept that he had anything to do with what was to come out of what he aired. He was simply in the right place at the right time to provide a platform for conversation and debate. He believed that the letters were at the centre of this, that they should be able to speak for themselves. By allowing Christine to speak and handling her story with compassion and sensitivity, he made hundreds of other Irish people feel brave enough to speak up. So many of the letters following Christine's interview are to thank her for speaking to Gay. Ireland had had enough of dark secrets. The world had opened up, and Gay's listeners were determined to make sure that Ireland was ready to modernise.

7

Northern Ireland

—

ONE OF THE GREATEST ASPECTS OF *The Gay Byrne Show* was its ability to reflect the mood of the nation. While whimsical and entertaining content was important to Gay, when it was needed, the show could also act as a forum to express national grief. As hidden social injustices were being uncovered south of the border, north of the border conflict ground on, bringing bloodshed, division and a sense of hopelessness for many across the island. Letters in the RTÉ archives following atrocities in Northern Ireland reflect the grief, shock, anger and sadness ordinary people felt at some of the worst moments of the Troubles.

Gay was often vocal in his outright condemnation of violence, and support for victims, on all sides, but it was not always welcome on air. He once said, 'There are several subjects guaranteed to send the letter writers hurrying to their desks ... But it is on nationalism and the North and associated topics that I get the most roastings.' Gay received this disgruntled and angry letter after he condemned the violence in the wake of the Enniskillen bombing in 1987.

Mr Byrne,

I was listening to your radio programme on Thursday morning last, at that part you devote to reading letters which apparently emanate from various listeners. One lady wrote about the situation in the Six Counties.

It was an entirely reasonable letter, yet it brought forth a tirade from you that was obviously unscripted and therefore could be taken at face value. Quite apart from interrupting your reading of the letter to make way for your own little remarks and quips, you finished by saying that you were fed up with all reference to that 'Cursed Place', the North of Ireland, or Northern Ireland, or whatever it was called.

The same 'cursed place', Mr Byrne, is part of my country. It is beautiful, friendly, courteous, and had produced down the years more than its quota of artists, businessmen and patriots. We remember Henry Joy McCracken, Roger Casement and, indeed, Michael Collins, who was elected as representative of a Northern constituency; we take it very hard, therefore, to hear it called by such as you a 'cursed place'. Moreover, I was privileged to serve in the Defence Forces. Never in all my time of service did I or any comrade ever apply such a term to our sacred country. It is irksome then to hear it so described by a jumped-up brat from the South Circular Road [...] whose favourite subject on the air is the femina abdomina.

I cannot sign myself 'Yours Faithfully' for you are of another faith altogether.

Speaking out during these tense times also came at great personal risk. A year or so later, Gay received a threatening letter, apparently from the Provisional IRA, who were upset at Gay's coverage of their campaign:

Mention the IRA once again and you've had it. We got them in South Armagh, so it should be child's play to get you. You'll be bumped off some night between Dollymount and Sutton and dumped in the sea. No excuse even if your ould fella and uncles from the slums of SC Road donned the British murderous uniforms. We have monitored you and in 1988 you have - at the taxpayers' expense - slagged the IRA 67 times. Your wife and two adopteds stand in danger too.
    Provo IRA

A well-earned picnic break during one of the many walks over the Bluestack Mountains in Donegal.

Unlike many people in the South who holidayed in the southern counties of the Republic, we spent our summers in Donegal. Dad adored Donegal: the place and the people. Time in the Rosses with the 'Donegal gang' were without doubt among his happiest. It was in Donegal that he was off duty and himself, always welcomed but never intruded upon.

During the Troubles, it was at times perceived as risky to drive through the North, and we were often encouraged to go to Donegal via Sligo. However, both Mum and Dad were not to be deterred, and so we always travelled to Donegal via Virginia; Cavan; Butlersbridge, where we would stop at the Derrygarra Inn for scones and tea before crossing the border; Lisnaskea; Enniskillen; Pettigo; and on to Dungloe in County Donegal. We knew the route so well: how the roads would change as soon as we hit the border, the red telephone and post boxes, Union Jack flags and red-white-and-blue kerbs lining our route; the smell of turf as soon as we crossed the border into Donegal, and the bouncy roads.

As children, we were both fascinated and scared by the border crossing. Our awareness and understanding of Northern Ireland was very important to Dad, and his explanations to us were always factual and without bias. But he knew the dangers, too. He always travelled separately from us, about 15 minutes ahead, on our pilgrimages to Donegal. Mum would follow behind in one of her succession of Renault 4s, suspension not a feature, Crona and I jolted about in the back by the bumpy border roads, giddy with a mix of nervousness and excitement.

There was always tension in the car when we approached the border crossing on what were known at the time as 'unapproved' roads. About 20 minutes before we reached the checkpoint, we would be instructed to stay quiet and still in the car. Mum would remind us that our car would probably have been spotted miles back by the army – the make, colour, registration and passengers all noted. She would explain to us that the British Army were

very nervous, especially of cars with southern registrations. The car would fall into silence as we got closer to the border. By the time we got there, Dad would have already passed through and given the soldiers our car details, explaining to them that we were en route to Donegal for holidays. We never knew if that made a difference or not, but it was our ritual and Dad's way of making it easier for Mum and us. What I do remember from those childhood border crossings was how upset Mum used to get at the age of the soldiers. Many were just teenagers, and clearly nervous. 'Every one a mother's son,' she would say, 'just doing a job they had to do.'

This letter was written by one such soldier, Stephen Cummins, who was killed aged 24 in a landmine attack near the Donegal–Derry border checkpoint in 1989. He had left behind, in England, an envelope which was to be opened if anything happened to him during his posting to Northern Ireland. Inside the envelope was a letter and poem.

I remember very clearly the day Dad read out on air the poem Stephen Cummins had included with his letter. I was driving through Dublin with my mother. The radio was on, as it always was in her car. My mum had been appointed to the Arts Council by Taoiseach Charles Haughey in 1989 and I was a teenager at school. We were driving into the city to her first meeting. She was dressed to kill and excited to start her stint on the Council.

I remember how our excited chatter stopped as we listened to Dad's slow reading of it; the silence in the air for a few seconds after; and how both of us quietly wept. We had seen so many Stephen Cumminses on our way through those checkpoints, many of them not that much older than I was at the time. It is the popular bereavement poem titled 'Immortality', written by Clare Harner. It was particularly moving, given the young soldier's age.

```
To all my loved ones,

Do not stand at my grave and weep,
I am not there, I do not sleep. [...]
Do not stand at my grave and cry.
I am not there; I did not die.
```

Fast-forward to 1998. The IRA had stunned the world by calling a conditional ceasefire just a few years before, bringing to an end a period of some of the worst atrocities of the Troubles. For the first time there was hope that a political solution to the conflict might be a real possibility. In April 1998, the Belfast or Good Friday Agreement was signed by all the main parties, except the DUP, and ringingly endorsed by referendums north and south of the border. It was a fragile peace, and it was shattered on 15 August when a car bomb planted by the so-called Real IRA exploded on Omagh's main shopping street, killing 29 people, including a mother pregnant with twins, and injuring more than 200 people, some maimed for life.

Just two months after the Omagh bombing, Dad and his team dedicated an entire *Late Late Show* to the survivors of the Omagh bomb. It remains a landmark episode, which didn't flinch from the grief, suffering and bravery of the people of Omagh but instead faced it head-on. My clearest memory

Gay speaking with Donna-Marie McGillion, a survivor of the Omagh bombing, during a *Late Late Show* special broadcast on 20 November 1998.

of that *Late Late Show* Omagh special was seeing Dad touch the cheek of 15-year-old Claire Bowes, who was blinded in the atrocity. She told him the last thing she saw before the bomb went off was her friends. She would never see again.

One year later, the people of Omagh invited Dad to come up and turn on the Christmas tree lights. Coming out on stage and seeing the main street packed with the people of the town, he was, for the first time ever, totally overcome. For the first time, the seasoned radio and television presenter had no words. On stage, as he was about to speak, he broke down completely and cried. Mum quickly took over the mic and said a few words so he could gather himself. And he did, remarking how overwhelmed he was that a town which had suffered so terribly just a year ago was able to come together to celebrate Christmas, and life. My sister, Crona, was with Mum and Dad in Omagh that day. It was the only time she or Mum would ever see him so overcome with emotion.

Dad was a man whose work in these decades ushered in so much positive change in Ireland, and he warmly welcomed each new turning point, from the decriminalisation of homosexuality and the introduction of divorce to the legalisation of contraception and gay marriage. However, one of his greatest joys was when peace in Northern Ireland finally became a reality. I vividly remember the emotion in his voice as he explained to me that he genuinely never thought he would be alive to see lasting peace in Northern Ireland. It was such an incredible accomplishment, he said, that if it could be achieved, anything could be achieved. His sentiments, we know, were echoed in homes across the island and the world.

To attempt to capture and appropriately frame in just one chapter the entirety of the conflict in Northern Ireland is a near-impossible task. But one particular event during this terrible time makes clear just what a remarkable achievement reaching peace was: the Remembrance Day bombing in Enniskillen in November 1987. It was one of the darkest hours of the Troubles, and the outpouring of grief and heartache, as seen in the letters sent to Gay in the aftermath, show just how much work had to be done, and highlight the courage of those living through it.

On 8 November 1987, a bomb exploded in Enniskillen at the town's war memorial during the annual Remembrance Day ceremony to remember those killed in war. A parade of soldiers was making its way to the town when the bomb went off. Eleven people were killed that day, ten civilians and a police officer. Sixty-three were injured, including thirteen children. A twelfth fatality, Ronnie Hill, died after spending the next thirteen years in a coma.

The IRA claimed responsibility for the bombing but said it had been a mistake; the target had been the Ulster Defence Regiment soldiers.

The youngest victim was a 20-year-old nurse, Marie Wilson. Marie's father, Gordon, had attended the ceremony every year for 40 years. This particular year, his daughter Marie had asked to go with him. His wife, Joan, was playing the organ in the church, so was unable to attend.

On *The Gay Byrne Show* just days after the bombing, Gordon Wilson told Gay his story. He and his daughter Marie had just positioned themselves with their backs to the wall of the town's reading rooms. About ten seconds later the bomb went off. They were instantly buried under six feet of rubble. Side by side in the darkness, they couldn't see one other.

He told Gay: 'I shouted to Marie and said, "Marie, are you alright?" She said yes. She found my hand and said, "Is that your hand, Dad?" "Yes," I said. I said, "Are you alright, dear?", and she said yes, but she kept shouting in between. Three or four times I asked her. She always said yes. I asked her the fifth time, "Are you alright, Marie?" She said, "Daddy, I love you very much." Those were the last words she spoke to me.

'I have lost my daughter and we shall miss her, but I bear no ill will. I bear no grudge. Dirty sort of talk is not going to bring her back. She was a great wee lassie. She loved her profession. She was a pet and she's dead.'

In the years that followed, Wilson's leadership and Christian faith were credited with helping to maintain calm after the atrocity. The 60-year-old draper publicly forgave the bombers and said he would pray for those who planted the bomb. He begged for no revenge. His remarkable words of compassion and forgiveness following the death of his daughter made international headlines. He would go on to campaign for peace until his death in 1995.

In the wake of the Enniskillen bombing and Gordon Wilson's famous interview, letters flooded in from listeners. Singer-songwriter Chris de Burgh was one of them, but instead of a letter he wrote a raw and emotional song, which he performed live on the show.

```
Standing at the War Memorial, children holding hands,
People getting ready, they're all waiting for the Bands,
And old men with their memories of comrades gone away,
Everybody gets together on Remembrance Day.
When the wild wind came without a word, just a sudden
flash of light,
Many there were taken, husbands, children, wives,
And a young girl in the ruins held her father's hand,
And her dying words were 'Daddy, I love you very much.'
```

The letters related to the Enniskillen bombing, and the Troubles more generally, show the wide impact on people of all ages and creeds, directly or indirectly. A number of letters on the subject come from young children, who should not be bothered by violence and the loss of life.

```
Dear Gay,
Although I am only 11, I would like to express my
feelings about Chris de Burgh's song about the bombing
in Enniskillen.
    Chris de Burgh's song finally made me realise the
horror of doing such a thing. I was also impressed by
the nurse who said 'I love you very much, Daddy', as I
feel it is the kindest thing anyone could have said. I
don't think that killing innocent people will ever get
us back the six counties. I hope that, sooner or later,
the IRA will see that they are killing innocent people
for their liking only, and that they will soon stop doing
this horrible thing.
```

Dear Gay, Although I am only 11, I would like to express my feelings about Chris De Burgh's song about the bombing in Enniskillen. Chris De Burgh's song finally made me realize the horror of doing such a thing. I was also impressed by the nurse who said "I love you very much, Daddy," as I feel it is the most kindest thing anyone could have

said. I don't think that killing innocent people will ever get us back the six counties. I hope, that sooner or later, the IRA will see that they are killing innocent people for their liking only, and that they will soon stop doing this horrible thing. As Chris De Burgh said in his song, I feel ashamed to be Irish on Rememberance.

Yours sincerely

While the Enniskillen bombing caused horrific and needless loss of life, it also unified people across the country, and they wrote to Gay to offer Wilson and his family support and prayers.

Dear Gay,

I have so often wanted to write to you, on various topics raised on your show, but now I feel I really must put pen to paper. I have been listening and watching, over the last few days, to all that has been said about the massacre in Enniskillen. When I heard Mr Gordon Wilson speaking with such eloquence and Christian love, I cried, and my children saw me cry, and I hope they will always remember.

I was confused by the turmoil of emotions within me, and needed to do something. So when Mr Wilson was on your show, some time later, I there and then sat down and wrote to him and his wife, just to reach over and hold them in their grief. Later that night, I was unable to sleep, and sat up in bed to think and pray about the whole event. As I began to pray, I wrote down my thoughts (a common practice with me) and I just enclose that prayer as my expression of grief as a fellow Christian, Catholic and mother.

Yours sincerely,

We Will Remember Them
They gathered in the morning, quietly reflecting,
On those who lay in death, killed by the violence of war.
And in one thunderous, explosive instant,
They had made that journey, across the great divide
To join those whom they had come to mourn.
From vibrant, throbbing life they moved
By an unlicensed hand
Into eternity,
To meet their God, their Father,
Father of Protestant and Catholic alike,
To dwell forever, side by side,
As children in their father's house.
O God of Peace and Justice,
God of Love,
Look down in pity on all of us,
Sons and daughters of Ireland.
And see the river of compassionate tears
Shed throughout this land
On this most dreadful day.
Forgive us our trespasses
As they so readily forgave their trespassers.
But deliver us, Lord, from this bloody and tormenting evil.
Amen

God of Love,
Look down in pity on all of us,
Sons and daughters of Ireland,
And see the river of compassionate tears
Shed throughout this land
On this most dreadful day.
Forgive us our trespasses
As they so readily forgave their trespassers.
But deliver us, Lord, from this bloody
        and tormenting evil,
                    Amen.

Letters poured in from all corners of the island — so many of them rejecting the violence taking place in the North.

Dear Gay,

I have just listened to the interview with the Enniskillen man whose daughter Marie died yesterday. How inadequate to send him condolences. I send him all the regret and sorrow and sympathy I feel. I know it's no consolation to this poor brave man who has been visited with such bitter tragedy. More important, I suspect, I send him my pledge, in public, that his daughter's killers have never and will never receive any support or sanctuary from me, that they do not represent me or the Irish people and that they betray everything our State stands for.

People are what make Ireland, and if we want Ireland to have any honour we <u>must</u> reject violence. Gay, people are afraid to stand out and publicly denounce violence. Hence the 'ambivalence' of Irish people. We all know what people fear, and it happened again yesterday. It's going to keep on happening, despite laws, police, or even capital punishment. The only way to make it stop is for each of us to swallow our fear and reject violence publicly and permanently, shout it from the rooftops.

This letter is my shout. May you get hundreds of thousands like it. Thank you for your own courage in publicly condemning violence. Keep up the good work.

Yours in peace.

-11-87

ENNISKILLEN +
IRA

Dear Gay

I have just listened to the interview with the Enniskillen man whose daughter Marie died yesterday. How inadequate to send him condolences. I send him all the regret and sorrow and sympathy I feel. I know it's no consolation to this poor brave man who has been visited with such bitter tragedy. More important, I suspect, I send him my pledge, IN PUBLIC, that his daughter's killers have never and will never receive any support or sanctuary from me, that they do not represent me or the Irish people and that they betray everything our State stands for.

People are what make Ireland and if we want Ireland to have any honour we must reject violence. Gay, people are afraid to to stand out and publicly denounce violence. Hence the "ambivalence" of Irish people. We all know what people fear, and it happened again yesterday. It's going to keep on happening, despite laws, police, or even capital punishment. The only way to make it stop is for each of us to swallow our fear and reject violence publicly and permantly, shout it from the rooftops.

Here is a letter from another young person, who also recognises Gay's reach through both his radio show and *The Late Late Show*, and his ability to make an entire country aware of an issue and get them talking about it.

Dear Mr Byrne,

I think the killing in Enniskillen was terrible. The IRA think that they are doing a lot for Ireland but they are not. I think it is scandalous. The man whose daughter died could have helped the patients if she was alive because she was a nurse. The IRA are doing nothing for Ireland. I am ashamed of them. There are eight children in this family and they all feel the same. I think the children of Ireland should not grow into that kind of violence. All I see on the Six O'Clock News is killing in the north, shooting and kidnapping in the south. I just want to say I am sick of it and so are my family and friends. I know that adults listen to your programme and watch your *Late Late Show*, so maybe they would like to know how a younger person feels.

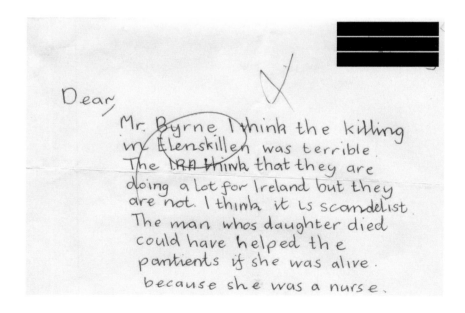

A young soldier pauses at the
Enniskillen War Memorial.

OUR GLORIOUS

1914-1918

1939-1945

Reading these letters, it is clear how upset and hopeless many people felt about the situation in the North. The letters are pleading, calling for an end to the atrocities that were being committed on all sides.

Dear Gay,

I know this is going to be an unpopular letter. But the more I have been listening and thinking the more positive I am that this should be said.

We have all been searching our hearts recently; revulsion, horror, it has all been so painfully expressed … but for all our wanting to redress this tragedy, for all our wanting to undo this evil, the root of the cancer is still there … namely the border around the North of Ireland … The North of Ireland, with its discrimination, its hate and its injustice … People petrol bombed out of their homes. Children taken in for questioning, beaten, abused, until they become another Dessie O'Hare, another Enniskillen bomber, another Bobby Sands, another tragedy of Ireland.

Don't tell me it doesn't happen because I hear the horror of the North every day on RTÉ.

How well for us that we live in a Free South, without armoured cars patrolling our streets, without the incessant noise of helicopters over our homes and the jeering of the RUC depending on where you live and who you are.

We must get rid of that border, because that is the cancer that turns a beautiful innocent child into a monster or just another tragedy.

Yes, it is possible to get rid of the artificial border, and it does not involve guns and bombs. It involves us the people, the people of Ireland saying to England, this is enough, you have said you will leave the

North when the majority says go … So name the day, the hour and the year, even be it in twenty years' time, so that we on this island can have peace.

With best wishes,

Dear Gay,
I know this is going to be an unpopular. But the more I have been listening and thinking the more positive I am that this should be said
We have all been searching our hearts recently; revulsion, horror, it has all been painfully expressed.... but for all our wanting to redress this tragedy, for all our wanting to undo this evil the root of the cancer is still there... namely the border around the North of Ireland... The North of Ireland, with its discrimination, its hate and its injustice... People petrol bombed out of their homes. Children taken in for questioning, beaten, abused, until they become another Dessie O'Hare, another

yes, it is possible to get rid of the artificial border,

Another letter asks Gay to programme a *Late Late Show* special, specifically about the Troubles. It is clear how many people saw the show as a force for good – a forum for open debate, discussion and education.

Dear Gay,

When I heard the first report on Enniskillen, I cried. I cried also when I heard the second, third, and fourth reports on the news that day. This morning I listened to Chris de Burgh's song and again I cried but this time I just couldn't stop. I sobbed and sobbed in the midst of my chores. My toddler came in and she became distressed on seeing my tear-flooded face.

I can't find words clever enough to express my horror, shock, and sadness. I've never used the word 'hate' very much but the people who planted that bomb must live [with] it every day. How can hate consume people to such an extent?

This hatred has been taught for years in our homes and schools. When the Troubles in the North began, we all read the autobiography of Bernadette Devlin. In her book she explained how she had learned her lessons in a convent and how a nun taught her to hate the British. I wonder where Dessie O'Hare went to school?

Gay, I think something should be done to clear up the differences between Protestants and Catholics. A *Late Late Show* Special could bring ordinary people ignorant of each other's differences and a panel of experts, on the screen into our homes, to explain the rights and wrongs on both sides. Please, please, please consider this - we must get together now or this island of ours is finished. We, the ordinary people of Ireland, can do this in spite of the terrorists.

We have a wonderful bond in Christ - we must come
together through Him - it's our only hope.
    Sincerely,

In addition to the letters, poetry was another form of creative expression that was
regularly sent to Gay. This letter writer had written an earlier poem to Gay some time
ago, which had been read out on air as part of a competition. This poem, however, is,
in the writer's words, 'a far cry' from the happier romantic poem they had submitted.

Enniskillen, November 1987
Blood is cheap
Its loss passes; dried in the November sun.
Tears are cheap
Their flow ceases; stilled in the November sun.
Life is cheap
Its strength weakens; cooled in the November sun.
And when the wreaths of peace are placed
On risen mounts of fresh earth
Will we forget this horrible waste?
These bleeding wounds in human hearts.
Oh no.
Let us forever and always remember
This doomed day in early November.
When seeds of lasting peace were sown
Amidst dust, rubble and limbs torn.
Let flowers upon these graves grow
Let those in Enniskillen know
That we, yes we, who are down here
Will have a house of peace built there.
A place where every one can come
And think of that November sun.
Where people silently can pray
We never forget that fateful day.

As Gay read out each letter on air, more and more came in response in the following days. When read together, one can feel the unsettling mix of anger and sadness experienced by so many people in the country, so many of whom wanted no involvement in the violence and loss of life.

Dear Gay,

I am incoherent with anger at those who call themselves IRA. Irish? 'Irish' should be struck from that appellation. I am filled with (Irish) shame and utter disgust. What do we call them? Even gorillas do not do these things. Is there any word of describing these 'vilest of the violent'? All the words I can think of have become common usage and tired by reiteration since the worst excesses of the Holocaust in the 1940s.

If these are beings fighting for a United Ireland - we don't want them, or their families, friends, associates or supporters in Northern Ireland. I don't anyway.

As I write, my anger subsides and I am filled with a devastating sadness.

With highest regards always.

Yours sincerely,

The Remembrance Day bombing in Enniskillen had the effect of unifying the country in grief and disbelief. While it would be some time before the country would see peace, the letters sent to Gay during this time show a people desperate to find some sort of resolution and bring an end to bloodshed and death.

Dear Mr Wilson,

It has taken me a week to find the words with which to convey to you my sorrow at the appalling loss of life and the injuries suffered by so many in Enniskillen last Sunday.

I heard you speaking on radio three or four times on Monday. I saw you on television, and each time I cried.

I cried with grief for you at the loss of your beloved daughter Marie. I cried for all who had been bereaved and those so terribly injured, and I cried with frustration and anger that fellow countrymen could commit such a heinous crime, ostensibly in my name.

These evil men do not, have never, and will never speak on my behalf. I abhor their deeds. Underneath this cloud of tragedy where there is so much suffering, I do see a ray of hope. The coming together of the two communities in Enniskillen and elsewhere to pray for the bomb victims and their families gives me hope, the long queues of people here in Dublin waiting to sign the book of condolences gives me hope, but most of all your Christlike acceptance of the terrible thing that has been done to you shines like a beacon, again radiating hope.

My heart goes out to you and all who have been bereaved or injured. May God comfort you in your suffering. My family will remember you all in our prayers.

Yours sincerely,

The letters Gay received following the Remembrance Day bombing in Enniskillen illustrate the overwhelming sense of helplessness and heartbreak felt by people throughout the country. Peppered throughout the RTÉ document archives are letters written by men, women and children all desperate to show solidarity to those living through the Troubles on the island of Ireland. So many letters after so many atrocities, and these few are just a snapshot of the feelings of a nation.

8

'The Love That Dare Not Speak Its Name'

—

A NUMBER OF YEARS AGO, my children were reciting some poetry for my mum and dad as part of their speech and drama practice. One of the poems they had to perform was 'Stop all the Clocks', or 'Funeral Blues', by the British-American poet W.H. Auden. When they had finished, Dad said to them, 'Did you know that W.H. Auden wrote that poem for a special friend of his?'

Dad's declaration was met with a silence from my children, before they quickly jumped from their seats to correct him. 'No, RaRa, you're wrong. It wasn't for a special friend. It was for his husband!' they informed him.

Dad smiled and turned to my mum. 'Did you hear that, Kay? Isn't that just wonderful?'

One of the topics regularly discussed on *The Gay Byrne Show* – and one which always caused strong emotional response – was homosexuality (as it was, at the time, almost exclusively referred to). All these years later, this reaction from my children – their total comfort with Auden's partner being a man – was simply amazing to my dad, who had known a very different mindset in Ireland when he first took to the airwaves. Over the following decades, Dad would bear witness to an astonishing and rapid, albeit not always easy, sea change in public opinion. In the space of a generation, Ireland would shift its overwhelmingly conservative views towards homosexuality, largely informed by the teachings of the Catholic Church, to an overwhelmingly liberal outlook.

Ireland in the 1970s, 1980s and even the 1990s was a hostile and unforgiving environment for its gay citizens. Same-sex sexual activity was not decriminalised in Ireland until 1993, following a lengthy campaign and legal battle, fronted by Senator David Norris and the Campaign for Homosexual Law Reform, which led to a European Court of Human Rights ruling, in 1988, that Irish laws prohibiting male homosexual activities were in contravention of the European Convention on Human Rights. In 2015, Ireland became the first country in the world to legalise same-sex marriage by popular vote.

Just six years before the European Court ruling, on 6 October 1982, Dr Austin Darragh, the radio doctor on *The Gay Byrne Show*, was on air covering a segment on the latent AIDS epidemic. The first cases of AIDS had been diagnosed in the United States in 1981, while the first case in Ireland was diagnosed in 1982. Little was known about the condition, but fear was widespread: one letter written to Gay concerning pub slops (page 28) suggests that 'unscrupulous' publicans could be helping to spread AIDS by pouring 'the remnants of some carrier's pint, who had slurped and slobbered over' it back into the barrel. Dr Darragh stated on air that, 'medically, it's unnatural for people to copulate in any way which is not utilising the organs which the Creator presented them with in the appropriate fashion'. David Norris, by that stage a well-known activist and campaigner, and a regular contributor to both *The Late Late Show* and *The Gay Byrne Show*, took

David Norris at the Dublin Pride March in 1993.

issue with Dr Darragh's theories and phoned in to the show to present his side. Gay barely says a word throughout the debate: he allows Norris and Dr Darragh to argue it out – yet another example of Gay knowing that his listeners were more interested in hearing what his contributors had to say than listening to him weigh in with his opinions.

Reading the letters and listening to the audio files on this subject in the RTÉ archives, when anything even resembling equality was still a pipe dream, is a sobering experience. They span the entire range of human emotion, and represent views from all sides of what was, at the time, a divisive and contentious debate: those in favour of equality, from gay people and the parents of gay people; and those vehemently against, where often out-of-context tracts quoted from the Bible demonstrate the deep-seated influence of the Catholic Church. In a later interview, Norris acknowledged that Dr Darragh's views chimed largely with the conventional belief at the time. Much of the outrage observed in the letters centres on the 'unnatural', 'disgusting' act of homosexual intercourse. One writer, in 1990, suggests that it wasn't homosexuality, as such, that was the issue but, rather, 'buggery'. In such letters, rarely is the individual – their own hopes, dreams and ambitions – given much consideration. And it's important not to forget that there are real people behind these letters. The letters selected here highlight just some of the pain and suffering inflicted on gay people by a country that did not want to acknowledge their existence.

While many people who wrote on other topics were content for Gay to know their names and addresses (he was often requested not to read these details on air, which he always respected), what's striking about these particular letters is that many are not signed at all. Such was the culture of silence that existed in Ireland at the time – homosexuality was consigned to the shadows, silent and unspoken about – that, at most, one comes across a 'Mr X', a 'Galway listener', a 'Clontarf mother'. Some people might think it unusual that Gay should have dedicated so much time to the topic of homosexuality. It was well known that he himself was a Catholic with a deep faith. But, as Norris noted, Gay 'followed his own conscience'. Gay knew that the people of Ireland wanted to speak. He knew he could provide a platform on which people felt enabled to speak – and he was going to listen.

Studio i/v with Ben O'Rafferty, solicitor on the legal situation vis a vis
osexuality

Now yesterday we spoke to David Norris, who very eloquently and passionately
spoke about being homosexual,xandxxtkexximxxixxxtiansxx. and all of
what that means for him. . .now we could on and on for ever about attitudes
and beliefs and prejudices and that sort of thing. . . but lets turn our
attention today to the cold hard facts of the law, and Ben O'Rafferty, who's
a solicitor with an interest in Constituional law, is here to explain
to us all about the law. . asin stands now
First of all what is the legislation which makes homsexual behaviour illegal?
(1861 Offences against the state Act, Section 61, outlaws
buggery, both for men or animals, and then a further amendment
the attempt to commit buggery or indecent assault. . . notice t doesn't
refer to women!!

So explain to me exactly what David Norris's Court Case was all about
(Took a case to the Euorpean Court of Human Rights, because ireland has
ratfied Convention on Human Rights, Norris said that this legislation
contravenes Article 8 and Article 14 of Act, intereferes with his rights
won the case.)and because we are a party to the Con

So what does that mean, is the Government legally bound now to change the
law?
(Not legally bound but considered very "bad form", govt held up to public
odium by other member states.

Now just clarify this. . . this has nothing to do with the EC or 1992 or
anything like that?
(No completely dfiferent insitution)

And what about this incitement to hatred law that there was such a fuss about
a few weeks ago, doesn't that specifically refer to homosexuals?
(Ironic, it foirbids you to write or say anything which will incite hatred
against Homosexuals, but it itself is still iellgal.

So what should the government do?
(Should repeal or amend legislation

Ok now we are giving you our listeners the chance to express your opinion
about this, we have a tele poll lined up for you. . .

This letter, from October 1987, written by a young gay man, shows just some of the loneliness and isolation experienced by gay people at the time:

Dear Gay,

I am a homosexual. I am 24 years of age, living and working in Dublin. I have always had inclinations towards my own sex, but I have never had a homosexual relationship, nor do I intend to have.

It is the inner feeling that is very hard to live with. As long as I can remember I have known deep down that I was not 'normal', in the accepted sense.

I am not looking for sympathy nor do I deserve any. I thank God constantly for the good health I have. I am grateful for having a well-paid permanent job. I have friends, a car and a marvellous family who, thankfully, are also in good health.

It is the private moments alone that I sometimes despair, knowing that I can never be married or have children. It is when I see everyone else of my own age group either married or going steady that I really fear for the future.

I have never told anybody of my position, and I don't think I ever will. If people could just think and try to understand and thank God for being normal. I am sure that in the future people will think to themselves that 'he must be, you know'.

The private hell that I go through is only balanced by thinking and appreciating the things that I have. I have never hurt anybody, so at least I haven't that on my conscience.

I would appreciate if you could read my letter.

Gay knew that his audience was listening to and corresponding with each other as much as they were to him. After reading out the previous letter, he received this one in response. Slowly it became clear that there were gay people in all four corners of the country suffering in silence – and they weren't as alone as they may have first thought.

Dear Gay,
I felt that fellow was speaking for me also.

I am of a similar age in a good, steady job, which I do very well. I have a nice home and am financially secure, etc. I am not what you would call happy with my life - content would be more appropriate.

When I was about 13 years old, I realised that I was different - my feelings for persons of my own sex were what is termed 'abnormal'. I read somewhere at that time that these feelings could just be a passing phase, that I should develop relationships with girls and pray to God for strength to overcome all difficulties.

With the knowledge that I could be a homosexual came the realisation that my very innermost feelings made me an object of disgust to the community at large, an embarrassment and shame to my family and damned to Hell by my Church.

Can you imagine the effect of all this on a boy of only 13/14 years? My early teenage years, which should be a happy and carefree time, were undermined by long periods of deep depression and despair.

Nobody prayed harder than I for a change to my feelings. I dated a countless number of girls and formed many long attachments. In later years, when relationships became more complex and physical expression more intimate, I had to break off many friendships with girls, with, I am sure, a mixed feeling of disappointment, hurt and embarrassment on both sides.

At 20 years of age, after years of despair, hope, prayer and lying to myself, I finally surrendered to the fact that I was homosexual and that was that. I grew up in a very Catholic family and would never do anything to hurt any of them. I never admitted to anybody my true feelings. I have never had homosexual relationships, or homosexual friends that I know of. I do not 'look gay' and am very interested in keeping fit and sports. Part of my job involves meeting the public in a social setting and I know many women are attracted to me.

What I am trying to express to you is the fact that a whole part of my life is one big lie. I have to lie and make excuses to girls who make advances in my direction, to friends who want to get me 'fixed up', to relations who jokingly ask if I am 'going steady' or when are you going to get married and give us a 'day out'?

I am not looking for sympathy from anyone, but many of your listeners will have sons or daughters who will grow up with feelings similar to my own. I hope they will be able to withstand the irrational hatred and pressures of our society. For the moment I am able to, but then half of my life so far has been spent doing so.

So many of the letters written by gay people grieve for the loss of milestones ordinarily taken for granted by their heterosexual counterparts – the thrill of a first kiss; experiencing a first love; finding a partner; not to mention marriage or having children, which, as noted in many of the letters, doesn't even seem to be a consideration for many.

One young man wrote powerfully about experiencing falling in love for the first time:

Dear Gay,

My life is currently in complete turmoil. The reason: I've fallen in love. I feel like a teenager (but I am in my mid-twenties). I did not think I could ever feel this way.

But what's the big deal about falling in love? What's all this about turmoil? I am a man, and so is the subject of my love. Since that first time we met my mind has gone through all sorts of contortions.

He is 'out'. I go to one of the gay pubs on and off. I am still a 'closet homosexual'. I am faced with a dilemma - do I now 'come out'? If I do, it won't be for [him], it will be for me.

I want my friends - who accept me for what I am - to go on accepting me when I tell them I am gay. But will they? How do I tell them? How will they take it?

I have always tried to live without putting labels on either myself or my friends. But here I am on the threshold of putting a major tag on myself. I am scared of the initial reaction and of the longer-term effect on my relationship.

I don't know where I am going with this. I just know that it is a case of now or never. I am meeting most of my friends this weekend and will tell them then. This time next week, I will either have strong friendships or none at all. What I don't want is to become isolated - polarised from my heterosexual friends.

I can't even think this letter through coherently. Advice from listeners who have gone through this would be appreciated greatly.

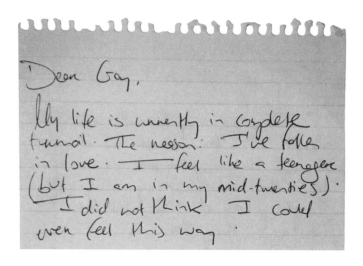

Dear Gay,

My life is currently in complete turmoil. The reason: I've fallen in love. I ~~feel~~ like a teenager (but I am in my mid-twenties). I did not think I could even feel this way.

While we don't know how things turned out, it is clear that this man felt comfortable enough to share this moment with Gay and the community of listeners that he had fostered. His consternation, though, is understandable when one considers the accepted beliefs of the time. As recently as 1990 – only three years before Ireland decriminalised homosexuality – the Archbishop of Dublin and Primate of Ireland, Dr Desmond Connell, had referred to homosexuality as a disorder, and something that could be 'corrected'. David Norris was, by this stage, an elected senator for the Dublin University constituency. He once again returned to *The Gay Byrne Show* to respond, criticising the senior clergyman for promoting and disseminating such damaging views. And yet despite the progress that had been made, Norris's appearance still caused a wave of criticism of him and his cause, and strong support for the Archbishop. People wrote letters in response, referring to homosexuality as 'abnormal' and a 'problem' that 'none of us would wish ... on our dear ones'. Such was the perceived support for gay rights on the radio show that one letter writer proposed the radio show be renamed the 'Gay Show', and as seen here:

> The Gay Byrne programme used to be entertaining, a family programme, but not any more. I think Gay is promoting homosexuality and I protest in the strongest possible terms for this to be coming over the national radio. I think the Archbishop is to be congratulated in not subjecting himself to Mr Byrne's questions on this subject.

Other people who contacted the show held similarly conservative views and supported the Archbishop. Ireland's history of silence can be seen clearly here – the idea, according to one writer, that 'gays are cultivated' and, as such, the topic should not be discussed. Many wished to ignore the issue, hoping, instead, that homosexuality was a phase that one could grow out of:

> It is a very brave stand to take to issue this statement. I agree with the Archbishop wholeheartedly. It could be a phase that a boy is going through, and if it is accepted they could fall into that way of life.

Reading these letters shows the pervasiveness of the Catholic Church at the time – how its teaching influenced all walks of life. In some letters, even gay people, who, for obvious reasons, largely disagreed with or felt oppressed by the country's widespread beliefs at the time, are seen to internalise the shame and disgust with which society viewed them.

An interesting and complex letter, written in 1993 – the same year that President Mary Robinson signed a bill fully decriminalising homosexuality – seems at first to be written by someone with strongly held religious and anti-gay views. However, this is not the case.

> Gay,
> I write this letter in response to the two letters that you read out on the GB Show last Tuesday […]
> I presume that they are members of some Churches […] I quote from a book called *Moral Problems Now*, written by a Jesuit and Paulist Father. In a chapter on the subject of homosexuality, I quote: 'Almighty God, in his plan of nature, intended that humankind be heterosexually oriented. The homosexual, regardless of the origin of his tendency, is afflicted with a disorder of nature.'
> Since both are young I cannot too strongly recommend them to seek help … If they have a medical card, they should go

to their doctor and tell him that they have a personality disorder and wish to be referred to a psychiatrist.

Many reasons have been put forward to explain the causes of homosexuality … One being the emotional development of the homosexual has not kept pace with the rest of his development. I completely disagree with those who maintain that gays are perverts. A pervert would imply that such people had turned away from a right way of conduct to a wrong one. They have not changed from anything. Heterosexuality has never been a reality for them, and they are not perverts but inverts.

Being male, I address my remarks to the young man in question. If he goes down that road of his sexual inclinations, his lot will be affair after affair. Some active, some passive, some long affairs, some short. Deceptions. One-night stands … Two-timing … Attacks by straights … What will happen to him when, as the years go by, he gets less attractive and finds himself being dumped for others younger and more handsome, not to speak of the reception he may receive from his family when he decides to come out of the closet.

In case people might think this letter is being written by a happily married man with a family the answer is no. It's being written by a middle-aged non-practising gay man, who has apologised to God for the moral mess he has made of his life and is determined to live what is left of his life within the framework of God's moral law.

I do have some black days of depression over the past misspent years, but I turn to the Joint Pastoral of the Bishops of Ireland, and there, on pages 37 and 38, I find compassion and understanding. May God bless them.

Or else they should admit that they only
~~support~~ ...iticus which support

Someone quoted Leviticus on homosexuality...
The book of Leviticus states that any
woman who has a period is unclean for
the length of that period. Anyone who
touches her is unclean; the bed that she
lies on is unclean and anyone who touches
it is unclean; the seat that she sits on is
unclean and anyone who touches it is unclean.
Anyone who touches anything on top of either
the bed or the chair is unclean, and
anybody who is unclean in this way is
himself unclean and must wash himself and
his clothes.

My point is that people who take Leviticus
seriously must do an awful lot of washing.

The Gay Byrne Show was a platform for all sides of any debate, and Gay felt it was important to air many different points of view. While the show received many letters featuring quotes from the Bible as reasons for the senders' opposition to homosexuality, it is important to note that not everyone felt this way. Many letters rebuffed religious quotes with readings of their own. For example:

> In relation to the letter referring to Sodom and Gomorrah and homosexuality, if you looked further on in the Bible there is also reference to the mixing of fabrics … that the mixing of certain fabrics is not allowed.
>
> I would like to make the point that we should not believe everything we read and if we did go by the Bible, then Gaybo would not be allowed to wear the nice shirts that he wears on the Late Late.

Even when covering such controversial topics, Gay maintained an impressive ability to balance heavy and light – a witty, clever remark could keep the show's tone entertaining while also serving as a withering put-down. In one letter the writer had once again quoted the Bible to illustrate the 'sin before God of homosexuality'. A listener to the programme called in with their reaction.

> Someone quoted Leviticus on homosexuality … The book of Leviticus states that any woman who has a period is unclean for the length of that period. Anyone who touches her is unclean; the bed that she lies on is unclean and anyone who touches it is unclean; the seat that she sits on is unclean and anyone who touches it is unclean. Anyone who touches anything on top of either the bed or the chair is unclean, and anybody who is unclean in this way is himself unclean and must wash himself and his clothes.
>
> My point is that people who take Leviticus seriously must do an awful lot of washing. Or else they should

admit that they only pick the parts of Leviticus which
support their prejudices.

While a significant proportion of the letters received on this subject, naturally, come from gay people, many straight people – particularly from younger generations – also wrote letters of support for their gay friends and family.

Dear Gay,
I am an 18-year-old student who happens to be heterosexual.

Why am I heterosexual? I don't know. It wasn't my choice to be born heterosexual, and I'm certainly not complaining. Nothing in the world could entice me into a homosexual life. If I was homosexual, the reverse would be true. Sex is only the smallest part of a relationship. A gay relationship is based as much on sex as a heterosexual relationship. What holds the relationship together is not sex but caring and friendship. What prompted me to write this letter was the fact that people kept ringing in and saying that 'God condemns homosexuality', 'look what he did to Sodom', 'the Bible condemns sodomising time and time again'.

Who is this God? He's certainly not mine. Those people could learn a thing or two about compassion if they bothered to read the Bible.

Every day, Gay's listeners tuned in faithfully. Much of Gay's audience were housewives and stay-at-home mothers: women who, because of their role and position in society, coupled often with living in rural areas, may not have seen anyone from one end of the day to the other. It could be a lonely, isolating experience. This letter shows just how important *The Gay Byrne Show* was to so many of these people: the writer here explains how simply hearing Gay's opening tune brings so much comfort.

It is interesting that in the archives today, a significant majority of letters received on homosexuality focus on gay men. Very few centred on lesbians. This letter tells a heart-warming story.

Dear Gay,

Can I let off a bit of steam? I'm here all alone. I have no friends that I can talk to. It was wonderful to switch on the radio this morning and hear your signature tune. I forgot about my depression for two hours. Thank you for that.

My world should have fallen apart four weeks ago. My daughter came home from Dublin, where she's working, and sat myself and her father down to tell us something. The first thing we thought was that she's pregnant, but no, she's a lesbian.

Up to that point she and her father didn't even communicate, but since this news came out their whole relationship changed. He hugged her and told her for the first time he loved her and she him.

I have thanked God since that day. Our home is a much happier home now. I can't explain it.

Thank you, Gay, for a wonderful programme. Thank you, God, for a wonderful daughter, who just happens to be a lesbian.

It is very moving to see supportive letters written by parents of gay children. The raw compassion, love and protectiveness evident in the letters from mothers spark huge emotion. While it is clear that they love their children unconditionally, the letters also say something about broader Irish society of the time. Many of the letters received – although supportive of their children – express fear for their future: the struggles they will face and the prejudice they will endure for daring to live openly as gay people in Ireland. At a time when homosexuality was still illegal in Ireland, the idea that gay people could marry or have families of their own wasn't even a consideration for many.

Dear Gay,

Further to the letter you had a few days ago regarding homosexuality, I have something to say on this matter. Firstly, at 23 years of age, my son came home one night and, finding me alone, said, 'Mam, there's something I've got to tell you and I hope it won't shock you too much.' I looked up at him and I shall always remember the pain and anguish in his face. I was sure he was going to tell me that he had cancer, and then he broke down and said, 'Mammy, I'm gay and I can't go on hiding it any longer.' I was devastated for him, as he is a highly intelligent, talented and deeply compassionate boy, who just adores children. We put our arms around each other and for some minutes we just wept in silence. I think we were both weeping for what would never be. And when we could speak again, he told me that he had been fighting this for years and, above all, it was not what he wanted to be. However, he was reaching a stage where he was coming close to a nervous breakdown.

I'll always remember him saying, 'Mam, it's going to be hard when people know, and I'll always be the butt of jokes' and, at that moment, I hated society for what it was going to make my son and others suffer, because there is, even in 1989, very very little understanding of this problem.

Over the past three years, I have watched his struggle and unhappiness in trying to come to terms and accept what he is, and I often think, 'My God, if people only realised the anguish and suffering these people go through, they would be slower to judge and realise that it is certainly not a choice one makes.'

I have tried in many ways to help him but basically the peace must come from within himself and now my prayers for him are that he will find happiness and somebody to love him. It no longer bothers me that it will probably be a man.

And may I say, finally, that the older I get the slower I am to make judgements on anything. You say it yourself, Gay, 'It may not be your problem today but who knows tomorrow?' Up to three years ago I would not in my wildest dreams have thought that it would ever be ours.

Sincerely

It is important to acknowledge that not all parents were so accepting of their gay children. Many of the letters that Gay received tell a story of gay people either not being able to come out to their family, or coming out to their family and then being rejected and ostracised by them.

A response to the letter that Gay read above tells a very different story.

Dear Gay,

This morning I heard the letter from the mother who has a gay son. I can tell you it brought floods of tears to my eyes. I am also gay. How I would love my mother to hold me and say that she loved me despite me being gay. You see, I have never had the guts to tell my parents or any of my family. I am now 35 and for the last 12 years I have lived a big lie. I think it's now too late to tell any of them. Somehow I don't think they would react the way that that woman did. That's a chance I'm afraid to take. I have never had a loving relationship with anyone - man or woman - in my life and now, at 35, I don't hold out much hope. Some days I can cope with it but most days I just despair for the future. Most of the time, I hope I will not be around when I'm 40 because I can't bear the thought of being old and lonely. I have got used to all the snide remarks at this stage. They don't hurt any more. I just long for someone to hold me in their arms and tell me they love me. God, how I envy that mother's son!

In 1991, Paul Gorry was a member of the Lesbian and Gay Youth Foundation of Ireland (LGYFI), a co-ordinating body for gay and lesbian youth groups and societies in Ireland. 'Back then, in the 1980s,' says Gorry, 'there was literally no information around to actually support a person coming out. You couldn't have a conversation with somebody.' Of course, it was a world without internet and instant access to information, so Gorry and his colleagues set up a phone line that young Irish gay people could phone for support and to have questions answered. The group put together a call-out and sent it to numerous radio stations and media groups throughout the country. 'Only one came back,' he says. 'And that was Gay Byrne.' Reflecting now, Gorry says: 'The fact that Gay Byrne actually took the time to read that was tremendous. That was the first time we were really being listened to and being heard. That gave us a great boost – that we are doing the right thing – that there is hope – things can change.'

This harrowing letter tells the story of a gay man at his very lowest.

Dear Gay,

I live in the west of Ireland and have spent the last number of years coming to terms with the fact that I'm gay.

I've always known there was something different about me but I secretly hoped that it would change and that I could lead a happy heterosexual lifestyle. God, how I tried! I dated many women hoping things would change and thought that I couldn't really make a decision till I was 28 and all my hormones had settled down. Well, they never settled, Gay. And I suddenly had to face the fact that I was gay and that it was pointless trying to change the situation.

Then the depression set in. I couldn't sleep … would spend days on end without sleep and then suddenly crash out for two days. My self-esteem sank to an all-time low. A week before my 30th birthday I had saved up enough sleeping tablets to commit suicide. I had my will written and a letter to my mother.

I will never know what happened that night. I had a bottle of vodka and the tablets sitting there and was just about to do it. I really wasn't afraid because I knew I wouldn't have to deal with it any more. But I decided to phone the Samaritans. I talked for about an hour to them and they gave me the number of Gay Switchboard Dublin. The next evening, I phoned them and I suddenly realised I was not on my own and I could get help.

That was two years ago. Since then, I've come out to my family. The most difficult was telling my mother. I don't think I've ever done anything as hard in my life. She really was upset but she just put her arms around me and told me she loved me so much and she was so proud I had the courage to tell her.

I also told some of my close friends. Some were very supportive. Others dropped me discreetly. But I must say that most of them have come around again, once they realised I was the same person I'd always been … The bond between mum and I has become so close. It's really wonderful and she is a tower of strength.

I feel that I've adjusted to my situation now. I may never meet a man to settle with. But maybe I will. I'll have to deal with it when it happens. I'm not a promiscuous person, but I also feel that I can't go through the rest of my life on my own. I honestly believe that I was born homosexual and that's the way I'll die. God must have had a hand in it somewhere and, some day, I'll have a few questions to ask Him. We all have to answer for our actions, I believe. But I don't think people burn for eternity. I have no intention of leaving the West. People here have their suspicions, which I neither confirm nor deny. I have a lonely lifestyle. But that's OK because I can accept myself now.

Sorry to be longwinded, but if it helps it's worth it.

...it never knew
...d that night. I had
...vodka and the
...g there and was
...do it. I really wasn't
...cause I knew I wouldn't
...deal with it any more.

...decided to pho
...aritans. I telled
...to them and th
...e number of Gay
...them and I suddenl
...was not on my ow
...cald get help.

always been...
mum and I has bec
It's really wonderful and sh
tower of strenght. I fed that
                                    sett

Dear Gay
I live in the
and have spent
years coming to
fact that I'm
I've
was some
but I s
change
a I
life

...them
...No mo...I do h
...mother as upset
...anything as I was upset me so
...really was upset
...her arms around me
...she loved me
...was so proud I
...to tell her
...my clos
...suppor
...Bt

Settled
settled, Gay
to face
gay and
trying to
Then
set in. I
spend days
and then su
two days. My
to an all th
before my 30th
saved up enay
to commit suic
written and a

When Gay first took to the airwaves in 1973, gay people all over Ireland were denied their identity – rejected and made to suffer in silence. It is astonishing to witness, through these letters, the sea change that occurred in Ireland over a relatively short period of time – that Irish society could change such conservative views and become liberal in the space of a generation. As with the other topics that Gay aired on his show, he would never say that he played an active role in shifting public opinion. He simply knew that people wanted to talk, and that he could provide a platform for them to speak, whatever it was they wanted to say. Indeed, this caller commended Gay for his fairness on the show, and Irish people more generally.

> I would like to compliment Gay on his excellent programme on homosexuality. I am very heartened by the balance in the programme brought on by the listeners and it displays to me clearly what I always believed, that Irish people in general are not reactionary and can be well balanced on any subject, given a chance.

I wonder if the people who wrote these letters back then could ever imagine what lay ahead. It's impossible to say what happened to them – some, sadly, might not be with us any more. While David Norris believes that Gay had great courage in airing these letters, covering issues that newspapers and other radio programmes shied away from, I believe that it took even more courage for these people to write to Dad in the first place – to share their stories and to let other people know that they weren't alone after all. Reflecting now even on this small selection of letters written to him, Dad's palpable delight at hearing his grandchildren referring so normally to W.H. Auden's poem for his 'husband' is, in his own words, 'just wonderful'.

Please forward.

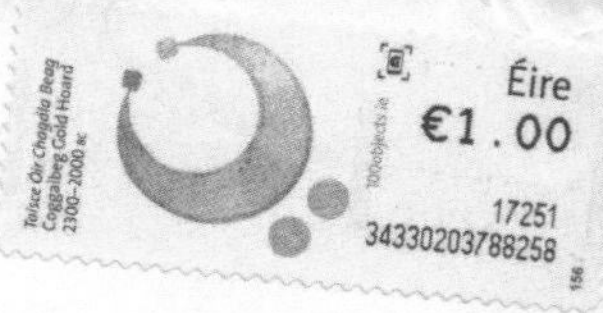

Éire
€1.00

Mr. Gay Byrne (Gaybo),
R.T.E.,
DONNYBROOK,
DUBLIN 4.

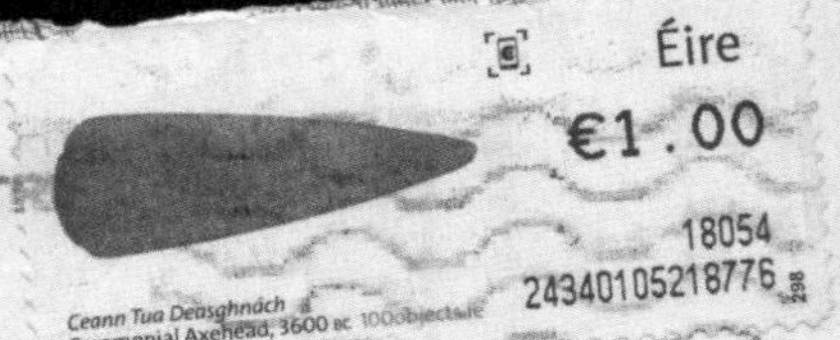

Éire
€1.00

DUBLIN MAILS CENTRE
26.02.18
21:20:47

Gabriel "Gay" Byrne
c/o R.T.E.
Donnybrook,
Dublin 4

DUBLIN MAILS CENTRE
06.02.18
20:05:04
17713283

Éire
€1

Polychroralhus
multiphilus
Bundún Tine Ealaine
Fireworks Aonmore

MR Gay Byrne
of RTE fame
DUBLIN

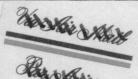

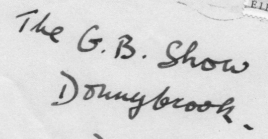

ÉIRE 32

The G.B. Show
Donnybrook.
Dublin. 4.

9

Letters of the Week

—

AS THE LETTERS CONTINUED TO flow in from listeners all over Ireland, Gay received a letter from one of his more prolific correspondents. Dubliner Robert Carty had written many letters to Gay since the show's inception. In 1988, he wrote a letter with an idea:

> Dear Gay
> A couple of ideas for your shows, which you might take on board … If a generous prize were given for the best/ most humorous/most touching letter of the week, say £50 or, better still, a couple of tickets for the *Late Show*, then the quality of letters submitted might maintain an even higher standard.
> Yours sincerely,
> Robert Carty
> PS. To start the ball rolling, how about a couple of tickets to the *Late Show* for this letter. No? Well, you can't say I didn't try, can you?

Carty's cheeky effort to nab two tickets to *The Late Late Show* is commendable. At the time, tickets to the weekly television show were like gold dust, with a famously long and fiercely contested waiting list. As teenagers, my sister and I were constantly asked when visiting friends' homes if there was any way that we could get them tickets, having exhausted their own methods. But Carty was somewhat surprised to receive a response to this particular letter from Maura Connolly, Gay's Special Assistant:

Thank you for your note, and well done. Great suggestion for the radio show. I have great pleasure in enclosing two tickets to *The Late Late Show* for yourself and Mrs Carty.

Carty's attempt paid off! And, perhaps more important, the Letter of the Week segment was born. It would go on to become a regular and much-loved feature on the radio show right up until its final broadcast in 1998.

Like many other women in the country at the time, Catherine Corless was a busy housewife, living in Tuam and raising her four children. This was long before Corless would become a household name, known and respected for her work in researching, compiling and uncovering information relating to the deaths of almost 800 young children at the Bon Secours Mother and Baby Home in Tuam, Galway. Corless had been an avid listener to Gay for many years. 'I loved the letters that women sent in,' she said of the show years later. 'Some of them would be amusing. I said I would love to do that ... When you'd be washing dishes or doing something or hoovering, my mind would be like, *What will I write?*

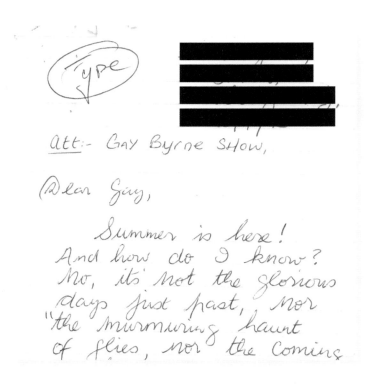

att:- Gay Byrne Show,

Dear Gay,

Summer is here!
And how do I know?
No, it's not the glorious
days just past, nor
"the murmuring haunt
of flies, nor the coming

Now, how will I put this together? Lo and behold I got an idea and I said, I'll write in for the craic. So, I did.'

In 1993, Corless sat down to write. Following the well-worn advice to writers, Corless wrote about what she knew: her children – along with a knowing poetic nod to John Keats.

Summer is here! And how do I know? No, it's not the glorious days just past, nor the murmuring haunt of flies, nor the coming musk-rose full of dewy wine that prompts of summer. No, no, Gay, it's the onslaught of mobile mania that has descended on our household once again. The what, Gay? Mobile mania!

Every old pram and pushchair and go-kart and bicycle and tricycle and trolley is pulled from its hibernation in sheds and bushes by our two boys and their assorted neighbours and friends. Axles, wheels, gears and frames are strewn across my lovely back lawn and are reconstructed into juggernauts and monster trucks. My well-kept lawn, patio and paved pathways have suddenly become Mondello Park and the sounds of summer for me will not be the nightingale, because I won't be able to hear him over the vroom vroom, beep beep, beep beep. (The latter is a juggernaut reversing, by the way, in case you didn't know.)

I'll probably spend summer once again resealing the tracks on the lawn, reviving shocked shrubs and replanting wherever crashes occur. I'm not complaining, Gay. After all, who am I to hinder the growth of budding grand prix stars? But I tell you, Gay, if I could get my hands on that fella who invented the wheel, I'd put his smile on the other side of his Grecian face, I can tell you!

Goodbye for now, Gay.

Mrs Catherine Corless

Radio Telefís Éireann

Baile Átha Cliath 4, Éire   telefón 01-693111, teleics 25268
Dublin 4, Ireland   telephone 01-693111, telex 25268

Dear

Gay Byrne would like to thank you for your comments and
contribution to the programme.

With the huge amount of poems, letters and other
submissions of recent weeks, we find ourselves
having to return an amount of material which might
otherwise find a place on the programme.

Please do not be disheartened at the return of your
submission, we simply have to make decisions from
among the immense amount of material submitted.

Yours sincerely,

_____

John Caden
Producer
Gay Byrne Show

sent to many w

The noise and chaos of young children during the summer is certainly something that I can relate to! Our own mum had an old cow bell, for which she was renowned among our neighbours. On the long summer evenings, we could be playing in any of the nearby gardens and the deafening noise of the bell ringing from outside the back door calling us home would supersede any laughter and mischief we were making. I recently found the old bell and use it to call my own gang now.

Corless sent in her letter and didn't think much more about it. One morning a few days later, though, as she was getting her children ready for school, *The Gay Byrne Show* playing, as always, in the background, Corless couldn't believe it when she heard Gay say on air: 'And what a beautiful morning to be reading a letter about summer from Catherine Corless.'

Corless was delighted. 'I was absolutely astounded. I couldn't believe it ... I roared at the kids, "Come in here!" ... We all stood around and we listened to every word. And it meant so much. I was absolutely thrilled for the day.'

Gay continued to receive a steady stream of similar letters. Listener Mary Wall aptly described the programme as a 'potpourri' – a mix of 'social comment, unusual stories, mystery sound competitions, music and requests to find a particular item'. Of the letters, she said, 'there were funny letters, heartbreaking letters ... sometimes hilarious, sometimes sad and sometimes sentimental.' Mary wrote a humorous, relatable letter to Gay in 1998, which was selected as Letter of the Week.

Providing some background to how her letter came to be, Wall explains, 'In younger days, I, unfortunately, was not blessed with a keen sense of direction, or, indeed, any sense of direction at all.' But Wall had been raised to always be polite and helpful. When she encountered two American tourists on Dublin's College Green, who were looking to get to St Stephen's Green, Wall was compelled to help them, despite her infamously poor sense of direction. 'I still have nightmares about those two lost tourists!' she admits, looking back today.

```
Dear Gay,
I've always believed that of the many afflictions one
can be born with, the worst one has to be a sense of
direction - or, should I say, lack thereof!
```

My reputation as a 'mystery driver' is widely renowned and at this stage I take no offence at all when friends mention 'get lost' to me if I offer to chauffeur them somewhere.

This unfortunate affliction does have its good points, I hasten to add, for I would never have realised the sheer beauty of this wonderful city had I not discovered most of it by accident. I have travelled the highways and byways of this fair city by default. As a southsider, I have been known to go to the airport via Naas, headed for Howth via Killiney, and tried with difficulty to reach the Blanchardstown Shopping Centre from Stillorgan.

As a teenager, one of life's simple pleasures was travelling into town with pals on a Saturday via the local 54 or 15A bus. My pre-motoring days were a lot less complicated, as the bus was much less likely to get lost.

Looking back I do recall with some embarrassment being stopped at College Green by two most polite but very obvious tourists who asked, in broad American accents, 'Honey, could you tell us how to get to St Stephen's Green?' Having always been taught to be polite and courteous I was reluctant to say I didn't know. What I did know, however, was that the 15A bus stopped right outside St Stephen's Green. As I was on my way home I quickly took charge of these two new friends and generously ferried them up to Terenure on a 54 bus and returned them to town on a 15A, where they could reach their destination. It gave me a wonderful sense of satisfaction to know I had helped someone, and was most gratified when the two visitors commented on how 'helpful the Irish were!'.

My affliction, I'm sorry to say, hasn't improved to any great extent, Gay, and, in fact, is considerably exacerbated by the daily appearance of parking cones, road works, diversions and one-way systems. As I'm never quite sure about the actual direction I'm travelling in, maps are somewhat superfluous.

Gay, what I want to know is: am I a 'lost cause'?

Yours sincerely,

Mary Wall

PS. I'm posting this at the Post Office in Terenure. I know my way home from there!

One of Gay's best talents lay in his ability to deftly and sensitively move from humorous topics to much more serious ones. Nowhere was this more clearly seen than in his Letter of the Week segment. In 1997, Fiona Marshall wrote to Gay about a miscarriage that she had suffered. Listening back to audio clips of the radio show, it is incredible how Gay is able to temper his tone, quietening those tuning in so that they would give this sad letter (and many others just like it) due attention and respect.

'I want to read you an extraordinary letter,' he says. 'Just to bring us all back to earth again with a bump ... And I had to read this letter twice, three times, indeed, before I realised what it was about, because the opening sentence says: "I am writing this letter I wrote to the baby I lost a few weeks ago." Then she enclosed the letter. And it says:'

'How old is he?' A lady in the park asked me today.

'Four,' I said, as I pushed my beautiful son on the swing.

'Oh, isn't it time for a little brother or sister,' she said.

She doesn't know about you. She doesn't know that you died. My tiny little baby. So wanted and so loved and so much needed. She didn't know anything about you. She didn't know anything about how your daddy and I tried so hard to make you. We were even receiving fertility treatment in Holles Street. After blood tests and smear tests and a rather embarrassing trip to the loo for your dad, eventually those two blue lines on the pregnancy test told us you were on your way, and that your shining light had fallen on us. You were hard work to make. Not like your big brother. It just took a romantic meal and a few [drinks] and he was conceived.

You were only nine weeks when your light went out. People told me I was lucky because it was so early on. I didn't feel lucky. You had little arms and legs, a mouth. And I even read in a pregnancy book that you probably had a tiny little tongue at that stage. Did you not hear me telling you to move when the doctor scanned me? Did you not feel your daddy's hand squeezing mine in an effortless bid to make your heart beat? But you were gone, but not forgotten. For there was no life left in your tiny body. They took away your tiny body. But I kept your soul. I know it's with me for I feel you touch my heart every day.

I turned to answer the lady in the park. I wanted to tell her about you. I want to tell her all about you. But I can't. It's too soon. Instead of that, I walk away. And I let my tears fall and pray that the answer is yes, one day soon, maybe one day, yes.

Fiona titled the letter 'My Shining Light'. The letter struck a chord with many listeners who had had similarly tragic experiences, and many requests were received to read out the letter again. As such, it gave Gay great pleasure when he received another letter from her almost a year later, in June 1998.

'Do you want to hear a little tearjerker?' Gay says. 'You do. OK, a little tearjerker ... It's titled "My Best Birthday Present Ever".' On air, Gay reads how Fiona's doctor 'promised her constantly that everything would be alright'.

'And he was quite right,' Gay says.

When I was eight, I wanted roller skates for my birthday. When I was twelve, I wanted a bike. When I was sixteen, I wanted makeup. And when I was eighteen, well, I wanted a fella. But this year I got the best birthday present ever. I got you. I watched you grow. I saw your little heartbeat. I saw the little arm buds that would blossom into arms, and hands and fingers and nails. You were a miracle before our very eyes. Only a month before I conceived you, I had lost your little brother or sister when I was only nine weeks pregnant. It hadn't been my first miscarriage, but we hoped it was to be my last. We hoped against hope that you would hang in there. And yes, you did.

We watched on the scans in amazement as you grew little feet and toes and everything else in the right place. We even got a photo of you yawning on one of the scans. You seemed bored with all the fuss, but we never got bored. I had a difficult pregnancy. But every night I placed my hand on my bump. And I talked to you. Remember the long chats we used to have as I lay up in Holles Street? I promised you I would be the best mother in the whole world. I knew you were a girl. And even though I told everyone no one believed me. Until at twenty-four weeks I had a scan. And I laughed when I looked at the screen. You lay there with your legs wide open for the world to see that you were indeed a little girl.

Overnight, your dad became the typical protective father. He laid down the law about what you were going to be able to do and what you weren't going to be able to do. He said you're not going to be allowed out until you're eighteen years of age minimum. Then we sat up in Holles Street and we laughed our eyes out, even though we knew we had a long way to go. At thirty-seven weeks, on my 28th birthday, and after a twelve-minute labour,

I got my best birthday present ever. After what could only be described as the most excruciating pain, you came. As I pushed you from my body, I felt exhilarated. I looked down and saw you take your first few breaths of life. You looked at me with your beautiful blue eyes and then screamed down Holles Street to let them know you had finally arrived and you wanted your presence felt.

I looked at your dad's face, overcome by the emotion of your birth. And I held you in my arms and I kissed your gooey head, overcome with love and the wonder of you. My Róisín, my beautiful little rose, given to me on my birthday, a day we all celebrate together every year. And every day I thank God for the baby I thought I would never have.

Gay loved that his listeners could share their happy, special moments with him as well as the difficult times. He loved to hear that whatever he had been talking about on any given day would resonate with his listeners in different ways. In 1994, Gay interviewed the novelist Brain Cleeve on his radio show.

Gay didn't realise until the interview that Brian was a member of the well-known Cleeve family, founders of the Condensed Milk Company of Ireland, who were most famous for the production of Cleeve's Toffee. The toffee, which came in a slab, presented kids and adults alike with the seemingly impossible task of breaking it into edible pieces. However, it was seen as one of life's simple pleasures. One listener, Mags Ó Dálaigh, from Sutton Park in Dublin, was listening to the interview at the same time. From her kitchen, she wrote this beautifully illustrative letter to Gay.

'This is a lovely letter. I really enjoyed this,' Gay says, before reading:

I just had to write you after the Brian Cleeve interview, because it stirred the most wonderful memories for me. Like yourself, I never knew he was from the famous toffee family. That's what I wanted to tell you about.

I went to school in Presentation Convent, Terenure. I had a friend called Irene. When the bell rang at four, we got up on our bikes to cycle home and the first stop was KCR. First, just let me set the scene: it's the '50s, April, May, beautiful weather. It was always beautiful weather. Cherry blossom petals everywhere, sleeves pushed up, socks pulled down, jumpers tied around the handlebars, overweight school bags falling off the carrier and Kimmage Crossroads, there it was that we discussed everything.

Now everything included the unfairness of school, the rotten homework, teachers, nuns, sex. Well, sorry, we called it the 'facts of life'. And I do remember a couple of facts we couldn't lay our hands on. For instance, what possible function could men have on this earth? And what role do they actually play in married life? Well, needless to say, Gay, when we found out, that kept us in conversation for a whole year! But the highlight of the stop was the purchasing of Cleeve's Toffee.

Now, as you know, Gay, there was a great art in breaking this toffee because it was next to impossible to break down the middle. So, Irene and I devised a very fair plan. If I cracked it, she got first choice. If she was going to get first pick, I was going to make sure I got the toffee to break down the middle. And this is where the ritual came in.

You had to find a very sharp gate post, a garden railing or the gable end of a house would do. With feet apart, great concentration and a prayer or two, we'd whack the toffee against the wall. You'd be amazed at how expert we became. Of course, next day it was her turn and I got first choice.

So, with a mouthful of toffee, we mounted our bikes again and headed for home. Not a word passed between us. Well, how could it? It was impossible to converse because this delicious, creamy, buttery toffee jutting out at peculiar angles just welded your teeth together. So what if it yanked your fillings out? It was great value, because it lasted all the way until we parted at the Submarine Bar. Irene continued up Kimmage Road West. I turned right through Crumlin village on home to Drimnagh.

Thinking back on it now, you can keep your Peggy's legs, your bull's eyes, your satin cushions. The Cleeve's Toffee was the king of them all.

I have no idea where Irene is now, but if she's listening: happy memories, Irene!

PS, I still have all the teeth. And they're in very good nick!

'That's the sort of letter I love to get,' Gay says, as he finishes reading it. 'One of those memories that, just out of that mention, you can suddenly visualise somebody in the kitchen going into a reverie ... And then maybe standing there, sitting there, for maybe an hour, gazing out in the sunlight and remembering those happy days ... It's lovely that you let us know that a quick mention evokes such happy memories.'

Many of the letters that were selected as Letters of the Week featured memories of idyllic and enchanting childhoods. Gay celebrated these moments when he could. These types of letters, which often spoke of happier times, were the perfect distraction for the many listeners who, themselves, probably had much to worry about: money issues, employment, and feeding and clothing their large families. Take this letter, which captures some of the contrast between innocent childhood and the harsh truth of reality.

Dear Gay,

I was sitting upstairs on the bus coming home from town when my attention was drawn to the actions of three giddy young schoolgirls. One of them suddenly jumped up, pulled her cardigan over her face and started to dance, to the wild amusement of the other two.

A while later, another girl took a ragged picture of a pop star from her schoolbag and the three of them began to tell the image on the torn magazine page how madly they loved him. Then they spontaneously burst into song and sang, with pride and devotion, their idol's latest hit.

The infectious laughter and tomfoolery continued all the way home. The sun was shining in the window, and they were having the time of their lives.

A man of middle years turned to me and complained bitterly about their 'bad conduct' and 'disgraceful behaviour' and said that he, indeed, would be having a word with the bus driver and they would be hearing more about it. But I had no wish to become involved. You see, it is too well I remember similar times when my friends and I were all young, when every moment of life was a joy to live and we laughed our way through carefree days.

Only recently, I had occasion to look at a snapshot of that period: two girlish faces looked out of it from the distant past, little faces brimful of anticipation and wonder. It is not an exaggeration to say that in the old photograph they stand together, side by side. Were they to stand beside one another today, all these years later, they would tell how fate, strangely, dealt them both the same hand, in that they each have lost a son in death.

Two girlish faces looked out of it in
the distant Past, little faces brimful
anticipation and wonder. It is not an exagg-
ation to say that in the old photograph
they stand together side by side. Were they to
stand beside one another to-day, all these
years later, they would tell how, fate,
strangely, dealt them both the same hand,
in that, they each have lost a son in death.
One little Boy was tragically killed in
a road accident, the other, a young man,
sadly grew tired of life. So, the carefree
days have well gone and the laughter is no more.
In my heart I longed to say to
that man on the Bus. "Let the young
ones have their fling" even the song says
"Every season has a time, a time

fooleny con
un was shin
ving the b
man of n
complained
duct' and
that h
word wit
hearing
become
ell I rem
y friends and I m
very moment of life was a g
nd we laughed our way through care—
free days.
Only recently I had occasion
to look at a snapshot of that period,

ous
ter and
d
m
road where I
full name and add
cond Boy I mention who died
Recent tragic suicide and I don't, for that
want to Bring it to a personal level.
Thank you.

One little boy was tragically killed in a road accident; the other, a young man, sadly grew tired of life. So, the carefree days have well gone, and the laughter is no more.

In my heart I longed to say to that man on the bus: 'Let the young have their fling.' Even the song says: 'Every season has a time to laugh, a time to cry …'

So don't be eager to draw dark shadows across young paths, because life unaided will most certainly see to that.

It is fascinating to see how many of the letters sent to Gay are, in fact, in conversation with each other – directly or indirectly. So many letters are inspired by other letters that Gay read out on air, which, in turn, spurred memories for the next writer, which they wanted to share with him and everyone else. This letter, a wonderful illustration, was similarly inspired by the image of schoolgirls on the bus.

Dear Gay,

Your letter about the two giggling schoolgirls on the bus reminded me of my own childhood and adolescence. I was just like them, and it was all thanks to two wonderful parents who had a sense of what childhood was: a garden, a river and the friendship of a large number of brothers and sisters. Not to mention the gift of music as well.

I am the second oldest of fourteen children. My father kept our half acre of ground at the back of the house covered from end to end with flowers and vegetables. We took organically grown food for granted and saw it as our natural birthright. Dad, a perfectionist, loved his garden and kept it in perfect shape. We children never damaged anything there. We knew instinctively that it was there for nurturing and a positive force in our own lives. […]

I could write a novel about my mother. […] She reared us against difficult odds and, as a woman, I know that her life was very hard so that ours might be happy. […] It is the wonder of my life that she lived through the rearing of fourteen children and still remains one of the sanest people I know. […]

With our good friends we spent the long sun-drenched days of our youth fishing, swimming, climbing trees and generally having a ball, oblivious of the future and the troubled world outside. We were quite safe there, as we had strength in numbers and no one ever bothered us.

A happy childhood helps to light the way through adult life. When I hear of the unhappiness of children caused by uncaring adults it makes me cringe. It must be awful to have no happiness to look back on when the grown-up world takes one by the throat. And it does take all of us sooner or later.

I'd like on behalf of all our family to thank my mother and father for a dignified upbringing, a lasting set of values, to carry us through adult life, and above all for allowing us the right to a gloriously happy childhood, the memory of which will live on forever.

Many of the winning letters featured similar quiet reflections, happy memories and personal victories – moments that, in the grand scheme of things, seem unimportant. But they were important to Gay, and they were important to those who listened to him.

Valerie Wade started writing to Gay in the early 1990s. 'His radio programme was the soundtrack of my mornings as I navigated the endless stream of family adventures,' she recalls years later. Valerie wrote frequently to Gay and, to her amazement, he regularly read out her letters. Just like Mags Ó Dálaigh, who wrote in following the Brian Cleeve interview (p. 219), Valerie had been listening to Gay while driving early one day. Gay had been playing Mícheál

Dad's infamous green jumper. Mum believed that it had been thrown out years before, but when she visited the studio for a surprise party for the twenty-fifth anniversary of *The Gay Byrne Show*, she realised, to her horror, that he wore it every day! Left on the back of his chair after the show each morning, it would remain there until the next day ... for years.

23-9-93.

Dear Gay,
A little story, lets call it "Journey beyond fear"
Chapter I.

_____

This September day, to all others waking up
to it, was like any other cold grey
drizzly September Monday.
It was not so for me.
My waking was full of dread. I moved
through the routines of morning like a feelingless
being, as if not knowing what was to come.
But I knew only too well what was to come.

I achieved the usual tasks, I know not
how, and all the while the innermost
parts of me, alert and stinging, ever
Mindful — only 3 hours left — only
2 hours left.
— Now it was time; — time to prepare;
time to vest myself in the garments
I had carefully laid out for the task
ahead.
Only moments now — ¼ hour at most.

Ó Súilleabháin's 'Oileán' and Valerie says that the combination of this stirring music with the 'frosty, pink sky and misty morning' transported her to 'some other place and time'. She wrote to Gay to thank him for that moment, and he read the letter on air.

'I was gobsmacked,' she says. As a busy mother of four, Valerie says that 'hardly a week went by when there wasn't something that I found I wanted to write about.'

In 1993, Valerie tackled a lifelong fear and learned how to swim, and she felt compelled to share her terrifying first journey to the swimming pool.

Dear Gay,

A little story. Let's call it 'Journey Beyond Fear'. Chapter One.

This September day, to all others waking up to it, was like any other cold grey drizzly September Monday.

It was not so for me.

My waking was full of dread. I moved through the routines of morning like a feelingless being, as if not knowing what was to come. But I knew only too well what was to come. I achieved the usual tasks, I know not how, and all the while the innermost parts of me, alert and stinging, ever mindful - only 3 hours left. Only 2 hours left.

Now it was time: time to prepare; time to vest myself in the garments I had carefully laid out for the task ahead.

Only moments now - a quarter hour at most.

Oh, mercy! A red light. Precious minutes preserved. Savour them - enjoy this welcome delay. A second red light. Be calm. Breathe … Breathe even deeper. This will pass and be over soon.

Oh no! A green light. Move slowly onwards - enter through those gates - they represent the realms of terror and somehow that ceaseless rain seems to hammer down and

compound my fear. The moment is seconds away now. There
is no going back. I am immersed in my lifelong dreaded
adversary - for thirty-six years I've managed to elude
it - but no more - it is now.

My first swimming lesson has begun!

Dad would have particularly enjoyed Valerie's letter because he had faced his
own fear of the water a few years previously. Maura Connolly organised swim
coach Arthur Morris to teach a gang to swim in a pool near RTÉ: Maura, and
Mary O'Sullivan of *The Late Late Show*, and John Caden of *The Gay Byrne
Show*. Also in the group were other well-known names at the time, June Levine,
Ivor Browne and the playwright Hugh Leonard, who subsequently wrote to Gay
and ignited a controversial discussion on adoption (p. 124). Every Thursday
night for three years, they would faithfully go to the pool. Starting off not even
being able to put their faces in the water, they learned all the strokes and even
some lifesaving skills.

It would have given Gay great pleasure, then, to receive another letter from
Valerie just a few months later.

Dear Gay,
You may recall a letter which you very kindly read out
on Wednesday 30 September last, wherein I described the
deep-rooted fear with which I attended my very first
swimming lesson.

The thrill of that first swim, without any armbands
or floats or swimming aids of any kind, will be with me
forever.

Not since I gave birth to my first child, 11 years
ago, have I known with certainty that I possessed what it
takes to take on myself and win. And I was a formidable
opponent when it came to swimming.

To cut a long story short, the lessons are ongoing
and each week further improvement, new skills. But the

absolutely best part of all is that there is now no fear of water. The water holds delight and relaxation for me now. The dreaded adversary of my earlier letter to you has simply evaporated and disappeared. The achievement of learning to swim can only be seen as a very small pebble dropped in a large pool of opportunity, and the ripples are still spreading.

So that's my story, Gay. I suppose by most people's standards it's very dull stuff. Hardly headline news. But as I heard once, one should never underestimate the value of one's own contribution. And if this small achievement can reach one other adult non-swimmer, and give them the hope they need to attempt the same, then the story will have been worth the telling.

At home, Crona and I were also the delighted beneficiaries of Dad's swimming lessons. Every week without fail, after swimming Dad would go to the small newsagent in Milltown, which sold rejected chocolate by the pound. He would get a brown paper bag full of sweets for us. We were always waiting for him at the door, welcoming the smell of chlorine, as, with it, came the bag for us to share out. Broken KitKats, chewy Maltesers, Snack bars that had missed the biscuit – you never knew what you'd get. We divided the bag sweet by sweet. Two little girls in heaven!

As with so many of the letters that Gay read, he remained mindful of the community of listeners in conversation with each other. While reading out letters on air often sparked national conversation and social movement, they also had a serious impact, felt on a personal level, on those who had written them.

Valerie's image of the small pebble dropped into a pool of opportunity, ripples still spreading, seems unusually prescient when read back today. 'The effect of having my simple words read out by Gay was enormous,' she says. 'That he thought what I had to say was important or interesting enough to broadcast was mighty.' It inspired Valerie to join a creative writing class at her local adult education centre, and she would go on to publish an anthology

Dad, like Valerie Wade, conquered his fear of water.

of creative work, as well as a children's book. 'Perhaps if it hadn't been for Gay, and his reading out my letters, it might never have been written at all,' she says.

Of course, not every letter selected for Letter of the Week celebrated such gentle moments or personal victories. Some contained darker subjects, and, as was Gay's trademark, he continued to use his platform to highlight some of the most pressing issues of the day – easily moving between light entertainment and serious discussion.

Ireland was still a relatively poor country by the beginning of the 1990s. With almost one in five people out of work, Ireland's unemployment rate was the highest in the European Union at the start of the decade. And while Ireland's fortunes were to change significantly throughout the 1990s, Gay was still concerned about what life was like on an individual level. Take this letter on the seeping influence of unemployment on a whole family.

Dear Gay,

Suffice it to say that this is the first time I have penned a letter to a radio programme. Unemployment - yes, that subject again - it won't go away. When one talks of the unemployment problem in this country, they can only understand its true implications for all concerned if one is its bed-fellow.

Let me continue. My brother […] is a victim of unemployment. Throughout his working years, through no fault of his own, he has lost several jobs. Nothing specialised, just ordinary jobs. In these recessionary times, places close, people are let go and sent home to rot in the privacy of their own homes.

He is one of our statistics - pushed to the edges of society. His confidence and self-esteem, needless to say, are at an all-time low. Having gone through a few interviews, all with a negative result […] he cannot take another no. So in a sense he has given up hope.

His days are filled in by reading, looking at television, making a bite to eat, going to bed and getting up the next morning knowing that in each day there is not a minute's variation from the previous one. He is not needed. The smiles that once were so common have disappeared in the turmoil.

Not only has life eroded his spirit but for us, his family, to witness the deterioration of a personality in such a way is something I can't even begin to talk about. So in a sense too, we are victims of unemployment.

A job, just an ordinary job - something to get up for in the morning - is this too much to ask for in the 1990s in this country?

letter of the week.

Dear Gay,

███████████████. Suffice it to say that this is the first time I have penned a letter to a radio programme. Unemployment - yes that subject again - it won't go away. When one talks of the unemployment problem in this country they can only understand its true implications on all concerned if one is its bed-fellow.

Let me continue. My brother ███████████████████ is a victim of unemployment. Throughout his working years, through no fault of his own, he has lost several jobs. Nothing specialised, just ordinary jobs. In these recessionary times places close, people are let go and sent home to rot in the privacy of their own homes.

He is one of our statistics - pushed to the edges of society. His confidence and self-esteem, needless to say, are at an all-time low. Having gone through a few interviews all with a negative result he cannot, ████, take another no. So in a sense he has given up hope.

His days are filled in by reading, looking at television, making a bite to eat, going to bed and getting up the next morning knowing that in each day there is not a minutes variation from the previous one. He is not needed. The smiles that once were so common have disappeared in the turmoil.

Not only has life eroded his spirit but for us his family to witness the deterioration of a personality in such a way is something I can't even begin to talk about. So in a sense too, we are victims of unemployment.

A job, just an ordinary job - something to get up for in the morning - is this too much to ask for in the 1990's in this country.

Yours sincerely,

███████████████

p.s. Please don't read out my name : _   - thank you.

Even as the years went by, *The Gay Byrne Show* never lost the 'town hall' culture of its earliest days – a place where people could share their story or point of view or ask for help from a wide range of listeners. Whatever the topic, whether it be quiet or pleasurable recollections, personal milestones, or more desperate pleas for help and support, a strong community of listeners had formed – a community who were there to help each other as much as they could.

10

The Gay Byrne Show Fund

—

OVER THE YEARS, MANY, many letters to Gay came from people in difficult circumstances who had no one left to turn to. People in dire poverty due to illness, tragic circumstances, separation, bereavement or unemployment. People supporting relatives or spouses in the grip of alcoholism or addiction or caring for loved ones suffering from chronic or acute health conditions.

In January 1984, Margaret and Larry McStay joined Gay in the studio. Their baby son, Colin, just 16 months old, had a rare genetic liver disease and urgently required a new liver. Colin needed a transplant by early April – but in 1984, liver transplants for children under 5 had only been performed on a handful of occasions, and only in the US. A transplant at a specialist centre in Pittsburgh was his only chance, the estimated cost to the family approximately £150,000. As the interview ended, these were Gay's words to his listeners:

'This is a child here who is positively going to die in the next year or so if this operation isn't done. And if it is done, he stands a 60 or 70 per cent chance. But it is unthinkable that he should not be given that chance. Unthinkable to his parents that he should not have that chance ... so please do the best you can for us, and we will keep you informed every day of what is happening, okay?'

The public reaction to the interview was unprecedented. Donations flooded in from schools, workplaces, community centres and building sites. Over £1 million was raised, some of which paid for Colin's operation, the rest put in trust for the benefit of other liver patients at Crumlin Children's Hospital. It also sparked the idea to find a way to channel people's generosity to benefit those most in need. And so, the Gay Byrne Show Fund was established. What's interesting about the Gay Byrne Show Fund is that there were no concentrated fundraising activities or efforts associated with it. Rather, the fund relied entirely on discretionary donations from Gay's listeners, prompted by the letters that Gay would read out on air.

The letters that Gay received tell of the slow creep of poverty: extended unemployment, unexpected funeral costs or emergency bills, which in turn could put people into rent arrears, or simply mean that they would not have enough food to put on the table that week. It was a continuous, spiralling cycle that, once caught up in, was almost impossible to escape – a story that is still, unfortunately, all too familiar today. When Gay read out these letters, his listeners responded by sending money in to the show. The majority of donations received consisted of relatively small amounts – tokens from people who often had very little themselves but wanted to help in whatever way they could after hearing Gay read out a letter or ask for help. Alice O'Sullivan, at the time a researcher on *The Gay Byrne Show* and heavily involved in the fund, remembers that most of the donations were 'usually accompanied by a wonderful letter'. Similarly, many people who had been assisted in some way by the fund themselves would, later on, send in something small to someone else once they had got back on their own feet. Alice recalls, 'Every recipient was extremely grateful and very often a Mass card was sent to Gay personally as a thank you. At the end of each season, he could have opened a shop selling Mass cards!'

By this time, the waiting list for tickets to *The Late Late Show* was famous. Every Friday evening before the show, Gay or his special assistant, Maura Connolly, would speak to the audience as they took their seats. They reminded audience members of what they already knew: that tickets to the show were like gold dust and that they had received them for free. It was highly likely that *Late Late Show* audiences also listened to Gay on the radio during the week and would therefore be familiar with the Gay Byrne Show Fund. As such, they were requested to dig deep and donate what they could to a person who stood by the studio entrance holding a basket for the fund. Often this was me or my sister!

As with so many of the topics aired on *The Gay Byrne Show*, what started small snowballed into a whole movement. Before long, the steady flow of donations meant that the fund was able not only to respond to individual requests for help, but also to take part in community events and outreach initiatives.

Some of the letters and the circumstances they describe are so desperate that they are almost beyond belief. Money in the fund was monitored carefully, and the team worked closely with community welfare officers and social services, among other organisations, to verify the needs of anyone requesting help. Once investigated, it was almost invariably found that these pleas for help were genuine, revealing an overlooked, but prevalent, group of people who were suffering silently and without adequate help or support.

Gay always went to great lengths to update his listeners on how their money was being spent and where it was going. Each time Gay gave an update, the fund would receive a fresh wave of donations and attention from people who wanted to help.

These show notes, from early 1989, give some good general examples of who the fund had benefited over the previous December.

> 'Michael': a deserted husband in Galway with five children.
>
> Mrs D.: married with three children, whose leg was due to be amputated just before Christmas and there was also an eviction order served on her.
>
> 'Susan': whose husband had just left her and her children for her best friend.
>
> Two days before Christmas, the social worker from Crumlin hospital rang requesting financial assistance for a family whose little boy had just died and they needed money to open the family grave.

Gay treated every request with the utmost respect – he often emphasised to his listeners that so many requests came in from people who 'find themselves in dire financial need due to circumstances beyond their control'. That he could do this – treat these people with the dignity they deserved, while simultaneously applauding and encouraging the continued generosity of his listeners – is testament to Gay's ability to delicately balance the dark with the light.

THE GAY BYRNE FUND

NOW CHRISTMAS WAS A VERY BUSY TIME FOR THE FUND AND AS I TOLD YOU BEFORE
WE WERE UNINDATED WITH REQUESTS LOOKING FOR FINANCIAL HELP.DURING THE
MONTH OF DECEMBER, WE MANAGED TO HELP APPROX FOUR HUNDRED INDIVIDUALS
AND FAMILIES THROUGH OUT IRELAND. EACH FAMILY AND INDIVIDUAL WAS CHECKED
OUT THROUGHLY WITH THE HELP OF VARIOUS SOCIAL WORKERS/PRIESTS AND G.Ps.
AS I AM SURE YOU WILL APPRECIATE MOST OF THE CASES WE DEAL WITH ARE
HIGHLY CONFIDENTIAL SO THE FOLLOWING ARE SOME GENERAL EXAMPLES OF THE
TYPE OF PEOPLE WE HELPED OUT THIS CHRISTMAS.................

1."MOLLY"....WHO FOUND HERSELF UNDER CONSIDERABLE FINANCIAL STRAIN AS
   TWO OF HER THREE CHILDREN WERE VERY ILL AND SHE WAS UP TO HER EYES IN
   BILLS.

2. "GEORGE"....WHO DISCOVERED HIS SON WAS A DRUG ADDICT...ALL THE MONEY IN
   THE HOUSE WAS STOLEN TO FEED HIS HABIT.

3. PARENTS OF SIX, SEVEN EIGHT CHILDREN WHO JUST DIDN T KNOW HOW THEY
   WERE GOING TO PUT ANY FOOD ON THE TABLE LET ALONE GIVE THEIR CHILDREN
   TOYS...HOW DO YOU EXPLAIN THAT SANTI HAS NO MONEY? WAS A QUESTION MANY OF
   THEM ASKED IN THEIR LETTERS.

4. A BIG CHEQUE WAS GIVEN TO EACH OF THE FOLLOWING AREAS...BALLYMUN,
   BLANCHARDSTOWN, BALLYFERMOT, RIALTO,DUNLAOIGHRE AND TALLAGHT.

5. WE ORGANISED SEVERAL CHRISTMAS TRIFLES TO BE SENT TO VARIOUS FAMILIES
   AROUND THE COUNTRY.

6. ONE HUNDRED CHILDREN WENT TO THE PANTOMOME IN THE JOHN PLAYER AND HAD
   A BALL.

ONCE AGAIN ITS THANKS TO YOUR KIND DONATIONS THAT WE ARE ABLE TO HELP THE
MANY PEOPLE WHO WROTE INTO US SEEKING FINANCIAL ASSISTANCE.

Even as Ireland's fortunes began to turn in the 1990s, the fund continued to receive requests from people and families in need. These show notes, from January 1990, give further examples of how the fund had been spent the month before.

'Molly': who found herself under considerable financial strain as two of her three children were very ill and she was up to her eyes in bills.

'George': who had discovered his son was a drug addict. All the money in the house was stolen to feed his habit.

Parents of six, seven, eight children, who didn't know how they were going to put any food on the table, let alone give their children toys. 'How do you explain that Santy has no money?' was a question many of them asked in their letters.

A big cheque was given to each of the following areas: Ballymun, Blanchardstown, Ballyfermot, Rialto, Dún Laoghaire and Tallaght.

We organised for several Christmas trifles to be sent to various families around the country.

One hundred children went to the pantomime in the John Player and had a ball.

The Gay Byrne Show Fund continued to help people right up until the show finished in 1998. By 1993, it was estimated that Gay and his team were receiving at least 50 letters per week just from people seeking some sort of financial assistance. Ninety-five per cent of [requests] we receive', Gay said in April of that year, 'come in from people who just cannot cope financially at the moment due to some upset in the home, be it illness, death, unemployment ... and then there is the added stress with communions and confirmations approaching.' Further examples and stories, as seen in the show notes of Gay's updates from this time, of people the fund helped include:

Six months ago, a young woman in her 30s was left widowed when her husband died suddenly, leaving her with five young children … Besides coping with the trauma of her loss, she also had to deal with the stress of knowing that her bills were mounting up. There was no way she could pay the funeral expenses, and her daughter's, communion was coming up … Well, we managed to relieve her worry somewhat by looking after the communion dress and help with the funeral expenses.

A social worker got in contact with us to tell us about 'John'. A young man who, five years ago, developed a very serious condition which has left him disabled … He was determined to move out of the family home. This he did, showing great courage, and once he found his flat he was starting from scratch … and so we were able to start him off by buying him a sofa and armchairs, for which he was absolutely delighted.

These are just some of the thousands of people Gay and his team helped over a 14-year period. These stories, however, were not outliers or unique. Spending just a little time reading through the actual letters that were sent to Gay reveals that these were, sadly, common and widely experienced circumstances that many people around the country had to contend with.

Many of the letters in the archives came from 'deserted wives', as they were called at the time. These women had been abandoned by their husbands and left to raise often large families and manage the upkeep of their homes by themselves, with no support from the men who had left them. For various reasons – including childcare responsibilities, lack of training, illness, and simply gender discrimination – it was almost impossible for some women to find work. They were dependent on the Deserted Wife's Benefit – a social welfare payment that, once all the week's most pressing bills had been addressed, left very little, if anything, for unexpected expenses or simple treats for their children.

Christmas was a particularly busy time for the fund: once people had paid their rent, looked after bills, bought food and attended to any other urgent expenses, often it just wasn't possible to put anything aside at Christmas time.

THE GAY BYRNE FUND.

NOW OVER THE LAST COUPLE OF MONTHS THE GAY BYRNE FUND HAS BEEN VERY BUSY.
ON AVERAGE WE RECEIVE AT LEAST 50 LETTERS A WEEK FROM PEOPLE REQUESTING
FINANCIAL ASSISTANCE OF SOME SORT OR THE OTHER...95% OF THE LETTERS WE
RECEIVE COME IN FROM PEOPLE WHO JUST CAN NOT COPE FINANCIALLY AT THE
MOMENT DUE TO SOME UPSET IN THE HOME BE IT ILLNESS...DEATH...UNEMPLOYMENT
ETC...THEN THERE IS THE ADDED STRESS WITH COMMUNIONS AND CONFIRMATIONS
APPROACHING....

HERE ARE JUST A FEW EXAMPLES:.
----

1. SIX MONTHS AGO A YOUNG WOMAN IN HER 30s WAS LEFT WIDOWED WHEN HER
HUSBAND DIED SUDDENLY LEAVING HER WITH 5 YOUNG CHILDREN...BESIDES COPING
WITH THE TRAUMA OF HER LOSS SHE ALSO HAD TO DEAL WITH THE STRESS OF
KNOWING THAT HER BILLS WERE MOUNTING UP,THERE WAS NO WAY SHE COULD PAY THE
FUNERAL EXPENSES AND HER DAUGHTERS COMMUNION WAS COMING UP...WELL, WE
MANAGED TO RELIEVE HER WORRY SOMEWHAT BY LOOKING AFTER THE COMMUNION DRESS
AND HELPED WITH THE FUNERAL EXPENSES.

2.A SOCIAL WORKER GOT IN CONTACT WITH US TO TELL US ABOUT "JOHN"..A YOUNG
MAN WHO 5 YEARS AGO DEVELOPED A VERY SERIOUS CONDITION WHICH HAS LEFT HIM
DISABLED... ████████████████ HE WAS DETERMINED TO MOVE OUIT OF THE FAMILY
HOME..THIS HE DID SHOWING GREAT COURAGE AND ONCE HE FOUND HIS FLAT HE WAS
STARTING FROM SCRATCH....AND SO WE WERE ABLE TO START HIM OFF BY BUYING
HIM A SOFA AND ARMCHAIRS FOR WHICH HE WAS ABSOUTLEY DELIGHTED.

Dear Gay

I am a deserted wife with four children. I'm living on £136 social welfare. My ex-husband spent a number of months in jail for trying to assault me with a knife. Since this offence, he is now barred from our house. Since then, my children are always in fear, ██████████ ██████. Hopefully we have put all that behind us now.

With four children at Xmas, money is always on a tight budget. With the Xmas bonus, I bought half a ton of coal. My children's allowance I use to pay my rent and I try as best I can to keep ends meeting. We buy all our clothing from sales of work and second-hand shops. At Xmas, the children like to be just like all children, and to have some new

This letter, from a 'deserted wife', explains the impossible circumstances she found herself in.

> Dear Gay,
>
> I am a deserted wife with four children. I'm living on £136 social welfare. My ex-husband spent a number of months in jail for trying to assault me with a knife. Since this offence, he is now barred from our house. Since then, my children are always in fear […] Hopefully we have put that all behind us now.
>
> With four children at Xmas, money is always on a tight budget. With the Xmas bonus, I bought half a ton of coal. My Children's Allowance I use to pay my rent and I try as best I can to keep ends meeting. We buy all our clothes from sales of work and second-hand shops. At Xmas, the children like to be just like all children, and to have some new clothes and toys.
>
> This year, as good as I try, I just don't have the extra money for them. Could you please help, Gay?
>
> Thanking you,

This letter comes from a similarly struggling wife, although her husband remains at home.

> Dear Gay,
>
> Some years ago, I wrote telling you of the circumstances of my marriage. My husband is a pillar of society, both socially and in our church. His stipend must always be the biggest and he subscribes to every charity … without a grumble. But as for home, where the charity should surely begin, he gives sweet damn all.
>
> One of my children some years ago needed surgery and, as he wouldn't be accepted in VHI because of his ailment,

I had to draw out the wee legacy that my late father left me to pay it. 'His nibs', of course, would not. He created such a fuss that I would rather be a prostitute than ask him.

He rejects our son as he is not up to his standards in appearance, dress, etc. Two years ago, I stole two pairs of jeans in Winston's for this lad and cannot pay it back. The worry of it haunts me day and night. I lie awake worrying.

I am begging you to read this letter. The jeans were £25.98 (£12.99 each pair). The generosity of your listeners is astounding. If you could pay this for me, it would be such a help. I am not asking for the money directly, hence I am giving you the name.

Please try to pay this restitution for me. I have no hope and will never again steal. It is not worth it.

Ireland in the 1980s was gripped by high unemployment. 'Unemployment in those days was widespread and devastating,' says Fr Peter McVerry. 'The worst part of it was that you didn't see any hope. You didn't see any possibility of getting a job.'

It was not just financial difficulties that arose from long-term unemployment; there was also the mental anguish and depression that can come when one feels completely hopeless:

Dear Gay,

My husband has been unemployed for the last seven years. He was on a course for a year. He has tried for countless other jobs, but to no avail. A labourer by trade, he can turn his hand to any kind of work if given the chance. He has just recently applied for seasonal work, so I'm praying maybe this time he'll be lucky.

We have three children ranging from the ages of ten down to my baby girl. I can relate very strongly with those people of whom you spoke. I fear also for my children's future. We try so hard to school them, keep them in books, copies and other items, which they require through the years and then, at the end of the day, a dole queue or emigration.

It's a very depressing existence when your husband's unemployed. I stress the word 'existence' because that's all it is. You're trying your best to get your family by from week to week (no luxuries whatsoever). I myself suffer from bouts of depression, as does my husband. He even once talked about ending it all, as did a close friend of ours because he couldn't cope any more, and leaving behind a wife and young family.

We are very much in arrears with our rent (over £200) and we're in debt with our water rates. I just can't seem to get out of this vicious circle I'm in. When it looks like I'm going to manage, something else pops up and I'm back in a black hole again. If the children need shoes or any kind of clothing, then I have to miss a week's rent and that's how I'm falling behind; the same with the ESB bill, so all I'm doing is robbing Peter to pay Paul.

It frightens me, Gay, because I've almost been evicted twice, only I pleaded with the County Council. I couldn't tell my husband that, for fear of what he might do, and I couldn't have that on my conscience. I cry myself to sleep at night. I'm only 31 years old and I feel I'll never know what it is to have a good time again, as we can never go out together as it's too expensive to pay a babysitter and we wouldn't have the money.

I try to get my husband to go out for a few pints, as it gets him out of the house and chatting to a few people, and perhaps keeps him a bit sane.

I've been given help from our local Vincent de Paul but one can't keep running to them. I get our dole money on Friday morning (£134). I pay a local shop some money off a bill I owe, do a weekly shop, pay ESB, fuel, TV, rent, and try to keep some money for during the week.

Gay, maybe you could consider helping us in some way with our arrears. I know I'd be very grateful and if there's anyone out there who'd have a baby's buggy that they'd like to donate, then I'd be very grateful indeed. It's done me good to get some of my feelings down on paper and I hope you'll get to read it on your programme.

Gay, let me say this, people on the dole aren't layabouts as a lot of people may think. It's the way of this country. We don't like having to ask for handouts but sometimes there's no other way if we want to survive. […]

I hope there'll be a light at the end of the tunnel for us and many more like us.

Your sincerely,

Of course, it wasn't just women who were struggling or writing to Gay. Many men, too, through no fault of their own, often fell between the cracks – often through either unemployment or illness.

Dear Mr Byrne,
I am just sending you these few lines to see if you can help me in some way.

As my income is only £37.50 a week, when I get coal and gas and electric, I haven't much left. I can't even get myself any clothes. I just get the odd item in second-hand shops.

I suffer from tinnitus, also a hernia. I am waiting to go into hospital after Christmas for surgery.

So, I do hope you will do your best to help me in some small way out of your social fund.

Gay always wanted to air all views and experiences – never to stoke controversy but because he viewed his role as a way of taking the temperature of wider society on certain subjects. Even the fund itself was open to debate and different opinions.

One day, Gay read out a letter from someone who was critical of people in receipt of social welfare payments – a sentiment still prevalent today. As always, Gay's listeners were listening as much to each other as they were to him.

Dear Gay,
This is the first time I have ever written to a radio or television programme but I felt I had to write in response to the letter you read out during the week.

The woman who wrote that letter stated that all the people who were going on shopping trips to Liverpool were receiving social welfare. Well, Gay, I was annoyed when I heard this.

I am married with three young children and my husband is on the labour. He has just signed back on recently, after being in hospital for three months. This woman has no idea what it's like to live on the dole. By the time I pay bills - the rent, the coal, the gas, the insurance, the electricity, etc. - there is barely enough to feed us, let alone take shopping trips to Liverpool, or even into Dublin city.

I am writing this to you on Monday, which is 'waiting day' for me. I won't post it until Tuesday, which is 'pay day', because I might need the money that I will spend on the stamp to buy a bottle of milk. That is what it is like living on the social welfare. There are no shopping trips across the water.

```
        Don't get me wrong - I would love to go on one of
these trips. I would love to be able to buy my children
nice things, instead of just looking at them in the
shops.
        Happy Christmas, Gay, to you and to all your team.
```

The letters preserved in the RTÉ archives make clear just how much of a struggle life was for so many people in Ireland throughout the 1980s and into the 1990s. Something as small as deferring buying a stamp to ensure you'd have money for milk highlights this struggle. They can make for uncomfortable reading, and it is impossible to fully understand the true lifeline that the fund gave to so many. While the fund helped many people through difficult times, it was also used to inject some joy into people's lives – small tokens to encourage, support and brighten the lives of Gay's listeners and their wider communities.

The Gay Byrne Show Fund often received requests for musical instruments and many of the show notes see Gay asking his listeners to donate old or unused musical instruments, as long as they were in good condition:

```
        Pianos: two are needed, one for a child with cerebral
palsy and the other for a really gifted 14-year-old whose
family just can't afford a piano for her.
```

In many ways, the Gay Byrne Show Fund was simply a development of the show's earliest days. When Gay's radio show first went on air, the show 'specialised in finding things for people' (p. 10) – second-hand furniture, unused goods, and services. The fund operated in much the same way – operating entirely on the goodwill and donations of listeners.

This letter, received by the fund's team, is from a teacher requesting a new accordion for a young boy. What might be considered a small act by someone could have profound effects on the person it was given to.

```
        I am writing to you in connection with a fourteen-year-
old boy whom I am teaching at present. He is almost blind
```

... [Would] the Gay Byrne fund [...] consider providing
an accordion for him? For the past few months, he has
been learning the concertina and has proved both able
and interested. It is, however, a long, complicated
(and expensive) instrument and, as he has expressed an
interest in the button accordion, it would, in many
ways, suit him better. The cost of a Hohner B/C button
accordion is approx. £365/£350.

I hope the Gay Byrne fund can consider the request
favourably, as it could greatly enhance the quality of
life of a very intelligent teenager whose horizons at the
moment are quite narrow.

It is clear, given how confident the teacher is that Gay's listeners will respond to the
appeal, just how generous they had been towards the fund by this stage, and that
they would support in any way they could.

Dear Gay,

I teach in the Blanchardstown area which is 100 per cent
local authority housing, an area of rapid development.
At the moment we have 400 pupils, which will rise to
500 by January '88. In spite of this, we have terrific
parents, interested in their children's advancement and
altogether a great community.

So, on behalf of the pupils of our school, we would
ask you, Gay, to appeal to your listeners. We are sorely
in need of a fairly good piano for our Christmas concert,
school choir, and as a teaching aid. Needless to remark,
the financial position of many of the families is such
that we cannot ask for donations for a piano. However,
we feel sure that your listeners can help.

Many thanks, Gay,

In 1989, the women of the Darndale Family Centre decided to take part in the VHI Women's Mini Marathon. The group of runners needed good shoes to train for and take part in the run, and so they wrote to Gay. The fund was able to purchase 25 pairs of Nike runners for the women taking part.

Also in 1989, Mark Barry, who uses a wheelchair, was a 14-year-old student at Saint Tiernan's Community School. The school was renowned for table tennis and Mark was a star player. Mark would compete against able-bodied players, but his wheelchair was bulky and heavy, which put him at a disadvantage. The students and teachers decided to fundraise in secret for a new sports wheelchair for Mark, one that was more agile, with better movement, so that he could progress in his sport and just improve his everyday life. Their aim was to raise £2,200 – a huge sum in those days. John Dillane, a teacher at Saint Tiernan's, wrote to the fund to explain their efforts. The fund was able to assist John with a donation of £300. Not long after, John and the students, unbeknown to Mark, bought the chair and presented it

Mark Barry playing in the 2007 European Wheelchair Basketball Championship.

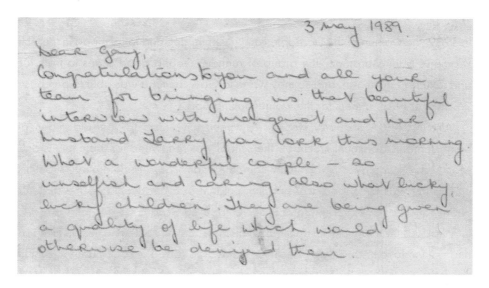

3 may 1989.

Dear Gay,
Congratulations to you and all your team for bringing us that beautiful interview with Margaret and her husband Larry har lork this morning. What a wonderful couple – so unselfish and caring. also what lucky lucky children. They are being given a quality of life which would otherwise be denied them.

A listener wrote in to express their admiration for Margaret and Larry Reid.

to him on the *Jo Maxi* TV show. Mark went on to compete at the 1992 Paralympics in Barcelona. Gay and the team loved to see how the fund could directly impact people's lives, not just in the moment, but setting them on course for a better future.

Over the years, Mum and Dad would often be stopped on the street by someone who had been helped by the fund in some way or other. They were always so happy to hear about how the fund had been there at just the right time – how things had improved once they had received that initial helping hand. Often people would tell them stories of how a cleared bill had lifted them out of a downward spiral, or how a musical instrument had changed the direction of their child's life and given them a new passion.

In 1987, a Cork couple, Margaret and Larry Reid, were the foster parents of two severely disabled children (as well as parents to their three biological children). Siblings John and Áine, aged 11 and 7 at the time, both suffered from brittle bone disease and could suffer broken bones and injury at the slightest knock or even by turning over in bed. Margaret describes the disease to Gay as their limbs being like a bridge with no steel. The children, who had been left in a residential unit, were entirely dependent on their foster parents. John had other disabilities in addition to his bone disease. The Reids had no car, which made taking the children anywhere very difficult. Both Áine and John

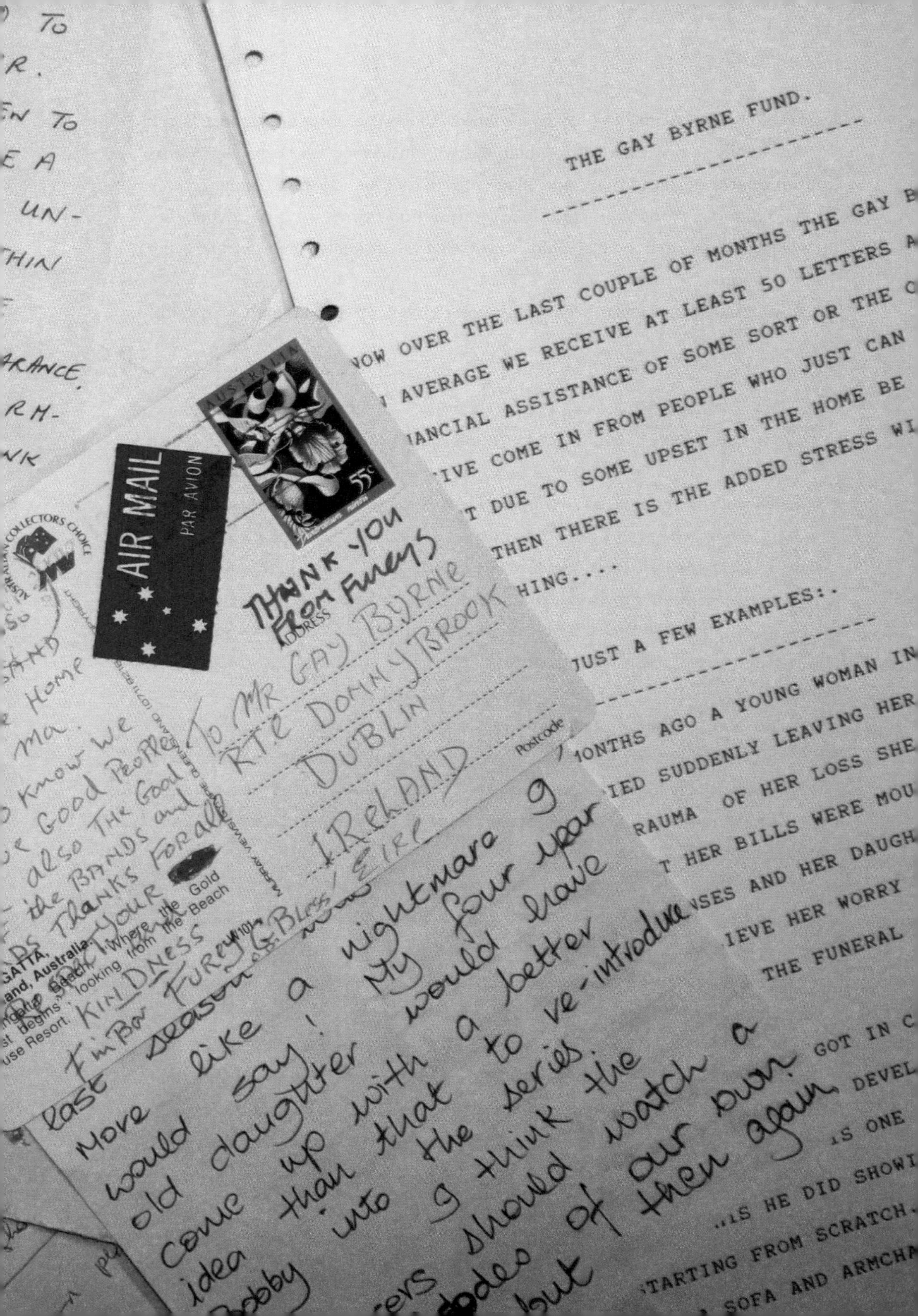

NOW OVER THE LAST COUPLE OF MONTHS THE GAY B
N AVERAGE WE RECEIVE AT LEAST 50 LETTERS A
NANCIAL ASSISTANCE OF SOME SORT OR THE O
IVE COME IN FROM PEOPLE WHO JUST CAN
T DUE TO SOME UPSET IN THE HOME BE
THEN THERE IS THE ADDED STRESS WI
HING.....

JUST A FEW EXAMPLES:.

MONTHS AGO A YOUNG WOMAN IN
IED SUDDENLY LEAVING HER
RAUMA OF HER LOSS SHE
T HER BILLS WERE MOU
NSES AND HER DAUGH
IEVE HER WORRY
THE FUNERAL
GOT IN C
DEVEL
IS ONE

...IS HE DID SHOWI
STARTING FROM SCRATCH.
SOFA AND ARMCHA

Postcard (handwritten):

AIR MAIL — PAR AVION

THANK YOU FROM FURCYS

To MR GAY BYRNE
RTE DONNYBROOK
DUBLIN
IRELAND
Bless/Eire

KINDNESS YOUR
Thanks ForAll
the Brands and
also The Good
e Good People
know we
Home
ma.

Finbar Furey G. Bless

Last season.

More like a nightmare g
would say! My four year
old daughter would leave
come up with a better
idea than that to re-introduce
Bobby into the series.
g think the
ers should watch a
todes of our own
but then again

were totally immobile. The Gay Byrne Show Fund was able to purchase a car for the family – a Mazda 323, complete with insurance and tax, which was presented live on air to the Reids, much to the listeners' delight. Listening back to the audio clips today, it's clear that Margaret and Larry were overwhelmed. 'It will just transform our lives,' said Margaret. 'It'll certainly open up a new life for the children.'

A short time later, Gay and the team received this thank-you note from the Reids:

Dear Gay,

My warmest greetings to you and all your staff.

I hope you will forgive me for not writing sooner but I was in a state of shock and only now feel capable of thinking straight.

I do not feel that I could ever adequately express my gratitude to you, your staff and all the listeners who contributed to your fund and made it possible for you to present us with this beautiful car, which is making life so much easier for us as a family. We have been able to do things in the last couple of weeks that we could not do for the last few years.

Áine's dream was realised when she went swimming last week. Unfortunately, she has broken her leg but at least she knows it won't be too long until she'll be back in the pool again.

John loves his car seat and is able to see all that is going on as I drive him in and out to school. I will not go on and on about all the difference the car has made, sufficient to say that it has truly changed our lives and we will be eternally grateful to you, one and all.

Our pleasure in receiving the car was made complete by the amount of good wishes bestowed on us by everyone. It seemed that everyone in Ireland was crying along with me when Alice handed me the keys for the car. We are just overwhelmed by the kindness and goodwill that have been extended to us.

I hope someday I will meet you so that I can shake your hand. I know that car was bought out of your fund, but there was a lot of thought, time and effort obviously put into the planning of the whole thing - so please allow me to thank you and your staff for that.

Today, the RTÉ archives contain a huge number of thank-you notes related to the Gay Byrne Show Fund. Through these, it's possible to see the real impact of the many donations that people all around Ireland had made over the years.

Dear Mr Byrne,
You will never know how happy we were to receive your cheque. My kids will be so happy Christmas morning and that means the world to me, just to see my kids' faces. I am so happy, you will never know. Only God will reward you.
Thank you sincerely,

Gay might also have been pleased to learn of his cross-generational popularity through this next letter!

Dear Gay,
I received your £200 gift this morning […] and I thank you very much. It is a big, big help for me. I just don't know who I'll pay a few pounds to to keep them off my back. What will happen when the *Late Late Show* finishes? There will never be another Gay Byrne, and believe it or not my teenage children idolise him. They'll always watch an hour or so before they go disco. Once again, thanks very much.
Yours sincerely,

Dear MR BYRNE
you will never know how happy we
were to Receve your cheque my kids
will be so happy christmas morning
and that means the world to me.
Just to see my kids faces. I am
so happy you will never know only God
will reward you.
        Thank you Sinceraly
        from ███████ family.

The fund helped not only individuals but community centres, local initiatives and other charities.

> I received the most generous cheque for £1,000 for the society yesterday. I cannot tell you how much we appreciate the money and the multiplicity of uses to which it will be put. Some examples: post-Christmas expenses, repair of storm damage - not everyone has insurance - coal - always a huge drain on our funds, examination and CAO fees […]

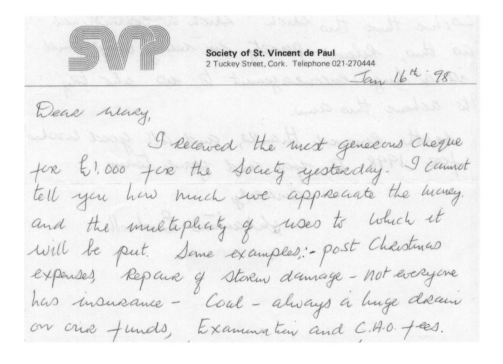

It seems that many of the letter writers had similar financial concerns to contend with: post-Christmas expenses, coal and heating bills, as well as CAO and exam fees – all issues that still trouble so many people today.

My dear Gay,

Thank you so much for the marvellous cheque I received from your friend on Friday last. It was a wonderful surprise and very timely, as we have post-Christmas expenses, and CAO and exam fees to deal with in the immediate future, as well as the ever-present coal bills.

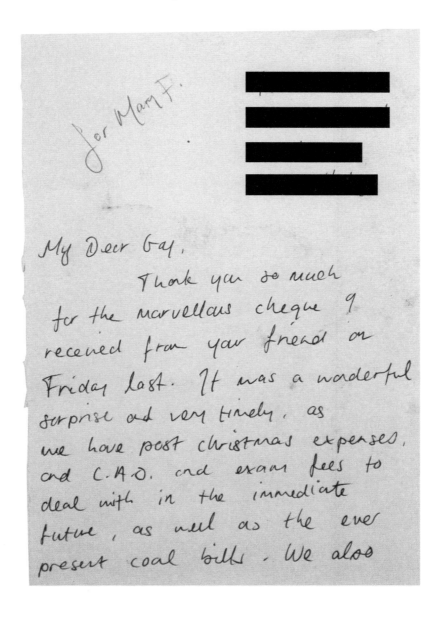

For Mary F.

My Dear Gay,

Thank you so much for the marvellous cheque I received from your friend on Friday last. It was a wonderful surprise and very timely, as we have post christmas expenses, and C.A.O. and exam fees to deal with in the immediate future, as well as the ever present coal bills. We also

The Gay Byrne Show Fund also donated to hospitals and schools around the country. Here is a touching letter from a young child attending Our Lady's Hospital School in Crumlin.

> Thank you for the lovely books. I am reading the one where Jiminy Cricket talks to us about the body. I must say that I did like the talk he gave about the heart, bones and liver. The talk he gave on how food digests was most interesting. But never mind that, I thought that the whole book was absolutely brill. I am sure I will enjoy the rest of the books whenever I get time to read them.

Regularly, people who had been assisted by the fund would, once they were back on their feet, send in their own small donation to the fund for someone else in need. It meant so much to many people and they did not want to let the kindness go unremarked.

> It was with surprise and tears that I received the cheque of £80 from the Gay Byrne Fund. A soul-felt thank you is all I can offer in reward for your thoughtfulness. However, I will consider the money as a boomerang loan I will repay, hopefully before this year is through, and you in turn will send the money out to another in need. Surely, one day, my weekly letter to the *Late Late Show* ticket office will be picked out of the tray, or whatever, and I will get the long-awaited tickets to the show, and I will make it my business to thank Gay Byrne personally for the consideration of his fund.
> I remain always grateful and thankful,

The Gay Byrne Show Fund remains a fondly remembered element of *The Gay Byrne Show* to this day. Looking back today, Alice O'Sullivan says: 'The Gay Byrne Show Fund was an extraordinary phenomenon within the show. Never before had a radio programme reached out to help people in need in such an organic, authentic way. The success of the fund was down to two things: the manner in which Gay read out each letter on air – it was done in an empathic, non-condescending way; and the generosity of the listeners. For every letter that Gay read out at least 50 letters came in with donations of £1 right up to £50.' In many ways, the Gay Byrne Show Fund highlights best what Gay wanted to achieve when he took to the airwaves. Looking back at the letters in the Gay Byrne Show Fund files reveals a wide-reaching network of people listening to each other, in conversation with each other and helping each other out in whatever way they could.

11

Legacy

—

THE THEME TUNE OF *The Gay Byrne Show* was synonymous with so many events in so many lives. Hearing it means something to everybody reading this book. Whether you were a child at the time, as I was, or an adult, hearing the familiar upbeat jingle again triggers memories for us all.

As a child, my dad was just that – Dad. Over the last two years, I have had the privilege of getting to know more intimately the public Gay my sister and I were less aware of as kids. As adults, Crona and I often joked with Dad that we associated hearing the show's signature tune with successfully staying home sick from school, whether the illness was real or fake. I'm sure we weren't alone in that!

So many times in my research, I came across footage or interviews I had not seen or heard before and I regularly got lost in it all for hours. It has been an emotional project, but truly an honour to have been asked to undertake it.

Dear Gay is about my dad's relationship with his listeners, and how they trusted him with their stories. They put pen to paper to express their hopes, fears and deepest secrets in an Ireland that was conservative – and often oppressive – in an era before email and social media. The letters to *The Gay Byrne Show* are a people's history of a very different Ireland; our dad, whether he realised it or not at the time, was the ringmaster of a national conversation that would in many cases change Ireland for the better. The letters featured here are only a small selection of those still conserved in the RTÉ Documents Archive, and my aim for this book was to curate a selection that illustrated how something as simple as a letter to Gay became a springboard for so many important national conversations.

The letters from listeners were such a huge part of the show – and yet they represent just a snapshot of it. Ireland was going through momentous social change, but it was not all sad nor hard. Listening back to the shows as I researched this book, I found myself engrossed in enthralling interviews and debates, hilarious calls from listeners and fascinating features by roving reporters. Many of these items were of their time but still relevant today, such as family members who had emigrated being reunited, live on air, with those at home.

I remember with particular fondness the production of *Oklahoma!* on the show in 1991. The cast comprised Gay and some listeners performing the musical live with the RTÉ Concert Orchestra. (The idea for this had stemmed from another successful musical competition called 'Singing in the Bath'.) Listening back, it made me giggle to hear him in his element, belting out those familiar songs, side by side with listeners from the length and breadth of Ireland. In 1992, the 'Messiah for Somalia' concert, organised by *The Gay Byrne Show*, was performed by choirs from all over the country to an audience in the Point Depot (now the 3Arena) and raised £250,000 for famine relief. And each Christmas Eve Dad would broadcast live from Grafton Street to huge crowds, with people singing songs, telling a joke or a personal story, or sending greetings to families abroad as they passed by. It was light-hearted fun, magical and happy.

In the days of mass listenership, *The Gay Byrne Show* was the nation's meeting point, a national front room where anything could happen and the conversation flowed, provoked by everything from national events to personal revelations.

Following his death in November 2019, many people wrote to us as a family, and to RTÉ, about Dad, and many others wrote or spoke publicly about him, sharing their memories and thoughts of, and about, him. By way of closing, I include a small selection of some of the tributes that were paid to him after his passing. Many of them reflect on what the show had meant to them, or their families, in the Ireland of the time; others on the impact his work as a broadcaster had on us as a society. Above all, the tributes that poured in after his death capture the greatest gift that Gay gave the nation: a safe space to talk – and listen – to one another.

'Up until then, most public debate in the country was conducted by politicians, priests or journalists, but *The Gay Byrne Show*, under his tutelage, moved it out into the people and hit the big social and sexual issues of the time. We talk of these things so readily now. Gay was great at this. He did all of these things, but we have no idea of the pressure he was under when he was doing them. He had unrelenting courage. One thing I would always remember of Gay was his courage.'

John Caden, Producer, *The Gay Byrne Show* (1979–1986)

—

'His thirty-seven years of full-time engagement with broadcasting did not happen by accident, nor without moments of editorial anxiety. It happened because of one man's talents, energy, capacity, resilience and personal qualities; because of the gifted programme teams who worked with him; because a public broadcasting organisation appreciated his talent, recognised potential and knew its responsibility; and because the audience knew instinctively that here was the genuine article, here was one who spoke to and for them, here was one who could, and did, change their lives. He made a difference in our world. And for that our society will be forever in his debt.

'It is given to very few to be welcomed into the bloodstream of the people, to be a source of oxygen to the life of the community. It is given to fewer still to be taken to the hearts of the people in the very particular way that Gay was. I often think that, without for a moment diminishing the importance and impact of his work on television, this deep relationship may have owed more to his radio work. He absolutely perfected the craft of radio and he fully understood the power of the medium. Perhaps it is to that quarter century of daily contact with him on radio that we can attribute the fact that he became lodged in our national consciousness in a manner that was intimate and personal for each one of us.

'Every morning, Kathleen, Suzy and Crona said goodbye to him as he headed off around Dublin Bay to RTÉ. Very much more often than not, he broke that journey for 7.30 a.m. Mass in the Church of the Sacred Heart in Donnybrook.

(Not bad for a man who was accused of denigrating all that was sacred, attacking Christianity and single-handedly undermining the foundations of the Roman Catholic Church!)

'Then, it was down to the concrete-lined studio in the basement of the Radio Centre. And in that strange, detached place, he sits down. He talks to himself. He plays music and makes phone calls. He is amused and angry, baffled and bemused, excira' and delira'. He talks and he listens. He listens. And oh, how he listens. With respect, with understanding, with empathy, with patience. He gives voice to people from whom we have not heard before. He listens with a quality of attention that women and men become able to tell their stories. To say things that have gone unspoken for long years. To rise above their fears. To share their concerns. To tell their truths. Just over twenty years ago, in the television programme *States of Fear* we heard such a voice – the first of its kind, the voice of a man talking to Gay Byrne on the radio in 1986 and breaking the silence about the pain of his childhood.'

– An excerpt from the eulogy by Bob Collins, Director General, RTÉ

—

'There is evidence that women of childbearing years were already, in their behaviour, ignoring or circumventing the custodians of the status quo – whether bishops, politicians, judges or doctors. Indeed, these latter groups were complacent and slow to sense the quicksand on which their authority rested.

'Byrne did sense it; in particular his intuition on where women stood on all of these hot topics seemed far ahead of the leaders of Church and State. [...]

'Retrospectively, it seems clear that he – and we – had the good fortune that he was the right man in the right place at the right time to play an exceptional role in late twentieth-century Irish history.'

John Bowman, *Irish Times*

—

'It was the letters, really, that opened up our society. We were an insular society up to then. Believing in everything. It was only if any of us went abroad that we discovered that there was another life out there. And we were very, very repressed and obedient and all of those things. But once you learn about another side of the story, it certainly opened our minds up. And it brought terror for some people who didn't want to change the status quo. And liberation for other people who at least had their voices heard.'

Maura Connolly, Special Assistant / Programme Executive,
The Late Late Show

–

'He changed Ireland quite a lot. He opened doors, and not just for mother and baby homes and people who got pregnant, but in every walk of life, and he wasn't afraid. He didn't care. He just spoke out. He spoke his mind. And I do believe that I would probably have gained some courage at the back of my mind somewhere because I was listening to this, day in, day out.'

Catherine Corless

–

'Byrne, it is clear, respected women. He gave them a voice. He championed them, on screen and off.

'Those who have worked with him say that it was the predominantly female audience that shaped his groundbreaking radio programme, and Byrne was just their conduit. If he was a feminist, he was an accidental one.

'Feminist or not, he gave Irish women a voice at a time when so many of the other institutions of Irish life would not. He addressed the things that mattered to them with an air of what's-all-the-fuss-about common sense – only partly belied by the glint in his eye that told you he knew this was telly gold.'

Jennifer O'Connell, *Irish Times* (2019)

–

The 'Messiah for Somalia' concert organised by *The Gay Byrne Show* in Dublin's
Point Depot on 27 September 1992.

'If *The Late Late Show* has waned in its power and impact over the last ten years, then the radio show has come into its own over the same period. This is where you get Gay Byrne at his most intense. Most of the time he is just superb. Gay reads a letter – it could be from a woman whose husband never talks to her, or a vicious attack on litter bugs, it could be about sex and teenagers. Sometimes he comments, sometimes he doesn't. Generally, he invites listeners to comment. Sometimes there's no reaction; other times the reaction is incredible.

'Then the discussion goes on for a week or so. Phone calls, letters, women giving their views, their experiences. Middle Ireland rearing its complex head.'

Colm Tóibín, *Magill Magazine*, (1984)

–

'Gay Byrne didn't see himself as a hero, you know. He wasn't up on his white charger doing something heroic. He was articulating the thoughts of everyday Irish people and giving them a forum, as opposed to the official view, which was the view of the Church, which was everlastingly sticking its noses into people's private parts.

'I think he's the male equivalent of Mary Robinson. I mean, Mary Robinson has her fingerprints on every single constitutional change that was made in that period. Gay Byrne is the same. He left his mark, by the interviews he did, by the letters he read out, by the people he spoke to.'

Senator David Norris

–

'His show was compulsory listening. And he did it in that friendly non-judgemental voice. He was interested in the stories he was reading out, and he was interesting. And he was relaxed. He was a wonderful presenter and I don't know his equivalent now. But as you think of Gay, and he's sitting back there in his suit, laughing, completely relaxed, and waiting for us to talk to him. He didn't even have to egg us along, or prompt us. He just sat down, and let the show go on. I have never heard his like since. [...]

'Not only did he open the airwaves to the nation, he opened the nation to his airwaves. He talked to us. He let us talk to him, and did not invade our privacy. There's been nobody like him before, during or since. It has not happened.

'Of course, a person can be unique, and he was unlike anybody I've ever known. I hope he was happy. And I hope he realised his own legacy and inheritance.'

Nell McCafferty

—

'Through his work in radio and on television he challenged Irish society, and shone a light not only on the bright but also the dark sides of Irish life ... In doing so, he became one of the most familiar and distinctive voices of our times, helping shape our conscience, our self-image, and our idea of who we might be.'

President Michael D. Higgins

—

'More so than any one individual, Gay Byrne represented modern Ireland and through his daily broadcasting on radio and television, he propelled this country and its people forward. In no other country can one individual claim to have had such a positive impact on an entire nation over such a long period. Ireland is a better country thanks to Gay's lengthy career behind the microphone at the centre of public discourse.

'He brightened and enlightened the lives of so many people through his broadcasting, his charm, wit, voice and wonderful command of the English language. His broadcasts were a public joy, a personal pleasure and comfort to so many.'

Joe Duffy

—

'Gay brought two unique gifts. He was able to see around societal corners and predict what the next emerging social, political, or cultural issue was, the new issue which needed to be brought to the public stage, whatever the ensuing controversy. Most importantly, Gay was a listener. He did not so much interview as allow his guests to almost interview themselves while he listened carefully, interjecting only to push them on key points.'

Moya Doherty, Former Chairperson of RTÉ

–

'Every week on *The Late Late* and every morning on *The Gay Byrne Show*, he was a conduit for all of it. He had an unerring instinct for all our mucky and sometimes marvellous linen that so badly needed to be aired.'

Róisín Ingle, *Irish Times*

"The Gay Byrne Radio Show" - 1981

Acknowledgements

—

RTÉ, THE AUTHOR AND THE PUBLISHER wish to acknowledge with gratitude the contributions and generous assistance of the following:

All the letter writers, whose correspondence features in this book or in the original RTÉ television documentary, *Dear Gay*, as well as many more, whose letters to Gay Byrne are conserved in the RTÉ Archives; All contributors to the original RTÉ television documentary, *Dear Gay*; The Byrne family; Maura Connolly; John McColgan; Doireann ní Bhriain; The management and staff of RTÉ Archives – in particular, RTÉ Document Archives; The production team responsible for RTÉ's original television documentary, *Dear Gay*, who have assisted in the creation of this book – in particular, Eanya Gallagher, Anne-Marie Staunton, Óisín McGreal, Roger Childs and Sarah Ryder.

For permission to reproduce photographs, the author and publisher gratefully acknowledge the following:

© Albert Fenton: 121; © Collins Photo Agency: 122; © Getty Images/Independent News and Media: 107; © Mediahuis Ireland: iii, xvi, 34; © Monty Fresco/Daily Mail/Shutterstock: 25; © PA Images/Alamy Stock Photo: 77, 175; © Pat Langan/ The Irish Times: 116; © Press 22: 266–267; © RTÉ Archives: xviii, 2, 8, 12, 13, 18, 21, 24, 32, 38, 42, 46, 52, 54, 57, 60, 63, 66, 70, 74, 78, 84, 86–87, 113, 114–115, 128, 131, 133, 136, 138, 141, 142, 143, 144, 152–153, 166, 170, 172, 173, 174, 177, 186, 200–201, 206, 207, 208, 212, 222, 225, 226, 232, 234, 238, 241, 251, 252, 255, 256, 263, 269, 273; © Shutterstock: 160; © Sportsfile: 250; © The Byrne family: x, xii, xv, 163, 230; © Trinity Mirror/Mirrorpix/Alamy Stock Photo: 14; © Sunday Tribune: 98; © SWNS/Belfast News Letter: 164; © Women's Way: 4, 5, 6, 7; Courtesy of Cleeve's Irish Confectionery: 218; Gareth Miller, Courtesy of Irish Queer Archive/National Library of Ireland: 182.

A special thank you to Sarah Ryder and Alice O'Sullivan for invaluable advice and guidance. Your firm belief that I could do this, and endless encouragement throughout, meant the world to me.

SUZY